Love Life

LOVE LIFE

*How to Make Your
Relationship Work*

Janet Reibstein

FOURTH ESTATE • *London*

First published in Great Britain in 1997 by
Fourth Estate Limited
6 Salem Road
London W2 4BU

Copyright © 1997 by Janet Reibstein

A catalogue record for this book is available from the
British Library.

ISBN 1-85702-621-7

Typeset by Avon Dataset Ltd, Bidford on Avon B50 4JH
Printed and bound in Great Britain by
Clays Ltd, St. Ives plc, Bungay, Suffolk

This book is dedicated to the memory of my parents, Louis and Regina Reibstein, and, most especially, to my husband, Stephen Monsell. In their own ways they have each taught me truths about love.

Contents

Acknowledgements

This book started through a series of discussions with colleagues and friends. Even today some raise their eyebrows sceptically when I mention this study. 'Right,' they say sardonically, 'and where did you dig up the single couple in the country who fits the description?' Or, 'Come on, do you really believe people when they say they're happy?'

Nevertheless, in the face of such scepticism, I found support for my ideas through early discussions with a number of willing friends and fellow psychologists. Chief among them at the early stages was Carol Gilligan, who read a primitive early draft and encouraged me to go on by saying, 'I don't think anyone's said this and it needs saying.' Lynne Murray also read a slightly later draft and gave me the benefit of both encouragement and further ideas, particularly around the theory of attachment. Jane Lichtenstein picked me up from the doldrums at a critical stage by suggesting a new way to think about organising the book. Her clarity and ingenuity were essential. I owe one great big chunk of the theory to my brother, Richard Reibstein, who read a very early draft and, smiling in disbelief, asked, 'Hey, what about pleasure? It's not all hard work, I'm sure.' I was stunned to see I had ignored what was right under my nose (although I think this was a side-effect of working with couples in trouble most of my career). It is no accident that my brother noticed the absence of pleasure; he is a source of tremendous pleasure, to me and to many others.

Vicki Barrass, of The Barrass Company, was in on the early stages too, believing enough in the project that she submitted, very early on, a proposal to make it into a series. Her clear and quick thinking, her optimism, energy, great sense of humour and gracious generosity have sustained me. She and her production team are joys to work with.

My chief cheerleader in this project, however, has to have been my agent, Araminta Whitley, who has nurtured it from inception, and who lived through ups and downs with patience, dedication and perspicacity. She has done more than many agents do – available through illness and birth, through moving house and jobs, she has helped sharpen my ideas as well as found a good home for them.

My editor, Sally Holloway at Fourth Estate, with tremendous good grace, managed to believe enough in the project to get it produced under very disadvantageous time pressure, and I am most grateful to her.

Finally, the experience of making the documentary series *Love Life* has been wondrous. The couples who participated have earned my deep respect and gratitude for their unstinting generosity and honesty. They have truly given of themselves, underlining the theme of love. The team at The Barrass Company, most particularly Martin Head, Lenka Thynn, Henriette Otley, Dan Owen, Vicki Curtis, Andrew Beint, and, of course, Vicki Barrass, were marvels of good humour, efficiency and professionalism. Most of all they were terrific fun, as were the film crew. This was truly a team effort, and the camera and sound crew, in what could have been an invasive and discomforting experience, were particularly sensitive and professional as we filmed. My thanks to all of them (who are too numerous to name, unfortunately).

My thanks also go to my husband, Stephen Monsell, and sons, Daniel and Adam Monsell, and to Monika Trentowska.

Without their cooperation on the domestic front, this book truly could never have been written.

Janet Reibstein
Cambridge, 1996

PROLOGUE

Scene One

I am sitting in the kitchen with Sue. She is talking to me about her husband, Mike, amidst the clutter of children's toys and homework and the preparation of the meal she and her husband of twenty years will make. Sue is weary and ill. She should have taken a prepared meal from the freezer, but she knows that Mike will appreciate that she did not. They have jointly cooked throughout their marriage. She looks forward to it; it partly defines their intimacy. They cook together like a dance - silently and cooperatively. At the end of a meal, both Sue and her husband comment to each other on the food gratefully and with pleasure: 'That salad worked, didn't it?' 'Good pasta tonight, Mike.'

Since most couples I know cannot prepare even two separate sandwiches in the same room at the same time, I have been struck by this seamless scene. On this occasion, Sue and I are talking before Mike gets home. He has been away for a few days, on business. He will arrive home, exhausted, but eager to relax with her in the kitchen. She hates it when he is gone. She tells me that her friends find her a bit 'neurotic', that she is 'too dependent' on him. Right

now, she anticipates his return with pleasure; she is trying
to explain to me that it is not 'neurosis' or 'over-dependence'
which lie behind her resentment of their separations.

'I could go on without him, I suppose,' she says, cutting
the carrots, 'but my life would be grey.' She turns towards
me, warming to her subject. Her face lights up as she mentions
Mike. This is the way people in the first throes of passion
look, I think to myself, when they utter their lover's name.
'My life is in technicolour when he is around. It's grey when
he's not. And he says he feels exactly the same.' She says
this, shaking her head in disbelief – she cannot believe her
luck, and is a little embarrassed. She resumes her chopping,
as if to say, 'Okay. That's enough. I don't think you really
believe it, anyway. You think I'm neurotic.'

When Mike arrives, after embraces, he brightens at the
chopped coriander and carrots, kisses Sue, and thanks her
for starting dinner. Then he begins his part, and their intimate
dance begins.

Is this couple from the real world? Most people do not
live happily ever after. Most want to; but unfortunately most
do not believe that they can.

Scene Two

I have come to collect my friend, Jenny, to take her and her
chronically ill daughter to their regular hospital appointment.
Jenny's husband, Rob, has told her at the last minute that she
cannot have their only functioning car today. He needs it for
a work appointment. She has rung me, enraged and desolate
all at once, to see if I can help. I arrive, expecting Rob to be
gone, but he is still at home and, despite my presence, is
haranguing Jenny for making him feel guilty. She is in tears
and offering a meek defence: 'Well, if you would buy a reliable
car for me, instead of a cheap wreck, this wouldn't happen
– you know that I have these regular appointments so I need
one . . .' At precisely this point, Rob takes his briefcase and

storms out the door – the door, that is, of a five-bedroomed house in the country, set in two acres. This couple have ample funds to buy a better second car.

Jenny has collapsed into tears, desperation compounded by intense embarrassment that this scene has unfolded publicly. 'Why is he so beastly to me? Doesn't he care about our daughter? Doesn't he want me to get the best care for her? I can't do anything right. It's been like this ever since, well, if I'm honest, ever since I had Daniel!'

Daniel is their second child, and he is seven, so we are talking about seven years of 'being like this' – a hell to live in, a punishment rather than a haven. How many Jennys and Robs are out there, having had white weddings filled with the promise of lasting love? We all know the answer: too many.

Introduction

This book takes the wish for a marriage like Sue and Mike's very seriously, instead of dismissing it as romantic tosh. (Note: In this book we will be talking about marriage and long-term cohabitation interchangeably[1]). It maintains that the intimate care-taking which characterises their relationship is the essential pivot for keeping romantic love alive. Our failure as adults to accept the need for as much emotional protection as we did as children can destroy our adult relationships. Failure to be protective is the key to why we meet so few Sues and Mikes. This book will show why they still see each other in technicolour. It offers a different way to think about marital love. In so doing, it maps out a path for the many to achieve what the few seem able to do: to remain in love and to maintain and develop a happy marriage.

Loving like this does not come easily, though we do not seem to realise this. Because romantic tales usually end at the wedding (whole years eclipsed by the lying words: 'and they lived happily ever after') and because there has been scant attention paid to the question of *how* to live in the increasingly complex state of marriage or long-term cohabitation[1], most people are naive about what it entails. It is not like the love you have for your children, you love them despite their bad behaviour (though you may disapprove of the behaviour). Yet your partner's bad behaviour can lead to the end of love. Mass murderers' mothers, appalled though they may be by their offsprings' crimes, may still devotedly visit them in prison, send them presents, trying to bring them comfort. Rapists' wives most often divorce them. To maintain love in marriage takes much conscious work, and this book devotes a good deal of space to how to do this.

The pivotal claim of my theory of love is that success in maintaining it stems from the fact that happy couples place concern for protecting each other at the centre of their lives, in much the same way that parents put their children's welfare at the centre. There are five key elements in the theory, which will be explored in detail throughout the book. These are: 'protection', which means treating each other with delicacy and welcoming a degree of co-reliance; 'focus', which means giving attention, time and energy to each other; 'gratitude', which means demonstrating appreciation and acknowledging your partner's value to you; 'balance', which describes a mutual give and take; and 'pleasure', which means enjoying your marriage and delighting in each other. The theory accounts for the durability of love across difficulties, over years together.

The elements of such a love transcend personality types, socio-economic backgrounds, education and careers. People of different backgrounds, temperaments and histories may be able to find matches across their differences precisely because of their ability to love in the way that this book will describe. Those who understand, and who live, the five essential factors manage to sustain love. First and foremost, these are people who recognise the necessity for a central, ongoing attachment, a partnership based on mutual security, loyalty and understanding, for both themselves and their chosen partners.

The point is that you do not have to come from a happy background or to have had a history of easy relationships before marriage or long-term cohabitation to find happiness. And, perhaps more importantly, a happy relationship can be made from one which has become unhappy. In other words, there is a chance for everyone, including those who have loved and lost it. All of the 'happy' couples in this book have experienced bad patches, ranging from clinical depression, unemployment and its accompanying misery, stillbirths and ectopic pregnancies, and crippling illness, to name a few. In the final chapters we meet a couple who managed to pull their relationship out of the lowest doldrums into a state of vibrancy through employing particular techniques and strategies. The one thing all these couples have had in common is that they once said they 'were in love'. For the last couple, as for Jenny and Rob and millions of others, this had faded into a memory, while for the others it had not. If you have once felt 'in love' with your partner but the love has faded, you also might use this new theory and techniques to regenerate your love.

It is only fair to say in advance that this book flies in the face of much current thinking. It is not quite the done thing to claim that people *should* need to depend on each other. Independence is not only a cultural ideal, it is one greatly espoused in particular quarters: both by some who say they speak for feminism and by much of the psychoanalytic establishment. It has entered the lexicon in many ways: maturity means 'standing on your own two feet'; to be 'launched'; to be 'your own person'. Ego psychologists in North America and psychoanalysts of the object relations school in Britain and Europe, each of whom have respectively dominated the language of development on either side of the Atlantic, talk about the process of maturity as one of 'separation' and 'individuation'. Not much value ascribed to interdependence here. The loud and, in the context of history, at one point necessary, support given to many women who left long-term relationships in order to 'become independent' and 'explore what it is to be your own person' was meant to correct the subjugation of women in marriage common in previous generations of relationships. Nowadays it may too often serve to obscure women's basic and highly developed need to be in relationship to one particular other; a need, shared with men, as precious to a woman as the need to understand her own tastes, talents and individuality.

I have been researching these issues for many years. For twenty years I have been both a researcher on the family, and a marital therapist and mediator, who also teaches and supervises other therapists. In this capacity I have seen, year after year, dozens and dozens of couples who have reached impasses in their relationships. Despite therapy, many relationships have ended. But a good proportion of these brave people (for it takes courage to bare your most private relationship to another, to pick it apart under the therapeutic microscope) have turned their relationships around, and have found the capacity to love each other again. This work has been alternately sad, when the pain of broken love explodes or seeps slowly out in front of you, and delightful, when you watch the lively bond of special caring between a couple as it gradually rekindles.

As much of my daily work is with couples in trouble, over the years I have repeatedly heard cries of the truly baffled. People feel slapped in the face by the failure of what they had thought love was going to be, and are embarrassed by this: 'Why can't he/she love me?' 'Why doesn't he/she pay attention to me?' 'Is it wrong to expect him/her to notice me/be kind to me/appreciate me?' 'Why am I always last on the list? Is it wrong to expect this?' And, 'I thought that's what love would be like. Was I wrong?'

Alongside hearing the stories of these floundering couples, I have conducted interviews with people who describe themselves as being in long and happy marriages with partners with whom they are still in love. These couples speak in marked contrast to those in marital therapy, and to the hundreds more I have studied indirectly through supervision, teaching, and to the roughly two hundred my co-author Martin Richards and I interviewed for our book about affairs[2]. From the testimonies of these two distinct groups – couples whose marriages have failed to make them happy vs couples whose marriages have succeeded in doing so – I have found the ideas and constructed the theory in this book. Although I have trained as a psychologist in traditional psychodynamic theory and methods, as well as in family systems work, out of the psychological theories on couples which have gone before, I have primarily been helped by two strands of work: first, attachment theory, a theory of development first set out by John Bowlby, and second, the theory of relational psychology which derives primarily from work by Carol Gilligan and researchers at Wellesley College's Stone Center. These two have provided a conducive ground on which to build my present model. Chapters 3 and 4 discuss these theories.

I have divided the book into two parts: Part One will provide a rationale for why, as adults, just as when we were children, we need protective alliances as the basis of marriage; Part Two describes in more detail how couples managed to stay on course and gives advice and practical hints on how to maintain protective love. In addition, throughout the book there are also some suggested exercises, to get you thinking about ways you yourself might make changes, to make your own relationship better.

The book includes accounts by couples who have managed to have transforming long-term love-filled marriages. It also includes accounts of couples who have not managed this. The contrast is informative. The two types are not two different species, but the same – human beings who have walked along different paths. The difference is that the route of the happy couples begins with a different set of guideposts – different assumptions about relationships and consequently different behaviour.

These couples were selected through self-definition. Most of the couples whose stories appear in this book answered advertisements for the five-part Channel 4 television series based on this book. Others were recruited by word of mouth. They nominated themselves in answer to the question: 'Are you happily married and still in love after at least nine years of living together?' Couples who have been encountered through therapy, or through interviews for my previous study on marital affairs, provide the contrast.

I was honoured to be able to interview intensively and get to know five couples intimately. These are the couples who are featured prominently in the television series. And brave these couples were, for the research conducted for this series demanded a very high degree of cooperation and candour. Out of 70 couples who described themselves as 'still happy and in love after at least nine years of being together', we selected twenty to interview in depth. These were from all regions of Great Britain, ranged in age from 23 to 76, were from all races and spanned the socio-economic groups. They had been together between nine and over fifty years. Out of that twenty, five were selected for intensive study. These valiant ones allowed cameras to be installed in two different rooms of their homes for two weeks. They were the subjects of interviews over two days (separately and then together) which were filmed. These interviews covered areas from the mundane ('how do you spend your time on a typical day' type of questions) to the most intimate ('tell me about what sex is like for you now' type of questions). The contribution made by these couples to this study cannot be overstated. In every case, the technical crew and the research and production team who got to know them were bowled over by the depth of their generosity and honesty. The stories in this book derive largely from the twenty interviewed for the series. The couples whose stories appear at the end of the chapters on protection, focus, gratitude, balance and pleasure appear under their own names. In all other cases, names have been changed and identifying details have been altered very slightly.

This book is meant to give hope to people whose relationships began in love, or who at some point found it, but who now seem to have lost the plot. If you are one of those people in one of those relationships, perhaps the stories of ordinary couples who have managed to keep love going, and the dissection of how they do it, will help you.

PART ONE

Why We Need Protective Alliances as the Basis of Marriage

CHAPTER ONE

Protective Love and Why We Need It

'When I got married I saw myself growing old with my husband. I thought we would always be together. I was 28. I knew even then we had a difficult relationship, but I thought it would only improve with time, as we learned to live with each other. We lived with each other, but I don't think we learned much. Instead of growing closer, we seemed to get further apart over the years. And when I got cancer in my forties, I thought, I don't want to live like this any more, because if I only have a few years left I want them to be in the company of people who love me, not someone who makes me feel even more vulnerable and hurt for being frail and dependent.'

Ruth is a woman of 45, a scientist and mother. She is composed and articulate. Tears are in her eyes as she tells me this. She has just visited a divorce lawyer and knows that she can financially manage on her own. It is not what she would have chosen, yet it has now become her choice.

What now, as we look toward the millenium, are our expectations of marriage? Throughout the western industrialised world marriage and long-term relationships are said to be in crisis. We have grown used to the familiar, persistent lament for its breakdown. Hand-wringing, simplistic prescriptions

('Back to Basics' and 'Family Values'), and punitive judgements (divorce is bad and marriage is good) accompany it. This is not surprising: in Britain we have the highest divorce rate in Europe; in the world we are second only to the US. The debris of many shattered relationships surrounds us, the fallout from the inherent contradictions in our ideas of love, which will be discussed in the next chapter.

For, under the barrage of publicity about bad, unsuccessful and broken marriages, the fact that most people not only still marry (and remarry), but that many stay married and do so happily, is lost. Moreover, on the heels of marriage is cohabitation; if we include long-term cohabitations which are like marriage, we could make this point even more emphatically. Alongside the lament, we still believe in love. We keep marrying for love with the expectations that our relationship will be like Sue and Mike's. But too often it turns out like Rob and Jenny's.

When Katie and Ed were each 31, they came to me for therapy. Ed was chronically late for work, characteristically tired and, although hard-working, unreliable. As he worked in a medical laboratory, this was perilous. In a last-ditch effort to save his job, Ed was advised by his boss to 'seek help' for his problems. And since his 'problems' were in his view caused by his marriage, both he and Katie showed up.

I could hardly believe these two were 31. While both looked haggard and prematurely lined, both also had the air of the teenagers they had been when they had met. Fifteen years and four children later, however, their marriage was a battleground. Katie recounted an adulthood marked by depression; Ed of resentment built up from years of periodically being yanked from work to tidy their house, look after their children, cook and shop while Katie lay immobilised by despair in bed. They spat venom at each other when not in tears.

Katie had married Ed both because she admired his competence and because she wanted to be part of his family, one of fixed patterns and habits. To Ed, Katie was wild, glamorous and full of sexual promise. Ed's life had been uneventful, while hers was marked by divorces, remarriages, precipitous descents into poverty and ascents into spending-spree recoveries, only to plummet once again into a life of sneaking out of rented flats in the dead of night to beat creditors. Katie had never made a bed in her life; Ed had known only routine. At eighteen they found themselves expecting a child; at nineteen they had their own house, thousands of miles from Ed's family. While a loving mother, Katie was never very good at schedules, or remembering to buy food or keep medicines in stock. The children became the couple's sole focus, as more and more problems arose around them. Child after child became the concern of authorities – the schools because of their absences and tardiness, the doctors because of chronic injuries and illnesses. Katie would fall apart in the face of demands that she be better organised. And so it fell to Ed to be so. Ed was unprepared for the sudden demands of maturity, but assumed all he could. He did so with increasing resentment. The veneer of glamour and sex had long faded. Katie was no fun, and had become overweight, sullen and slovenly. Ed, ever competent and reliable, grew nasty and snide. This was not what either had bargained for.

Most of the first few sessions were spent on recriminations. After these the tears came. 'You don't love me. You never did. If you loved me, this and that would never have happened'. Both complained. What was 'loving me'?

It was, according to each, 'showing that you could see that I was in trouble'. It was 'listening to hear that I was in over my head'. It was 'stopping to take me in, in some way'. It was 'showing that you could see I had gone out of my way to do something for you'. It was 'showing that you could see that I was trying my best – perhaps I needed help to do more'.

Both were unable to *say* anything like this during the marriage. Because they could not say these things, both expected that the other would instinctively know, would somehow divine what was needed, in the way a mother reads her infant's cries. But while infants cannot speak, grown-ups can. These two, like so many others, did not have the words, buried too deep. They needed a protective alliance. Unexpressed, unacknowledged, they corroded into resentment and anger. Moreover, without saying it, each partner could develop the false belief that, though he or she was someone capable of being hurt, the partner was not. The myth of the *in*vulnerable partner, the partner who is a rock, strong and untouchable, is permitted to develop. One year later this couple separated.

The widespread destruction of relationships such as Katie and Ed's shows just how desperate a state we are in. Chief in evidence is that one in two marriages ends in divorce. A very large proportion of our children will have got through childhood experiencing marital breakdown and remarriage at least once. The documented costs to children, parents and society of this pattern are enormous.

Further evidence of the decline in the institution of marriage is seen in the rise in the number of affairs, especially among women; and in the decline of the importance of the couple itself in family life as the relationship between parents and children has risen in pre-eminence. Moreover, nowadays people are beginning to abandon marriage as a legal form (we have seen for the first time, in this decade, that the number of marriages being contracted has fallen, although statistics from the US show that this trend is beginning to flatten; however, people who have been married before seem still to be remarrying). More and more people are trying co-habitation instead, perhaps in an apparent attempt to institute a still different form of emotional and sexual commitment. The currently available data, however, suggest that these forms are merely replications of marriage, without legal status, and are more tenuous as lasting arrangements than legal marriages[1]. People are looking for answers, yet not quite finding them; people are striving to find the key to maintaining a happy and successful relationship.

More evidence can be found in the fact that most people – even those who stay married for a lifetime together – find themselves in relationships which they commonly deem 'just all right'. According to some research[2], this is the expected state of long-term marriages. After a long time people settle for less and less.

As a long-married friend said to me recently, 'Sometimes I look at my husband as if through the eyes of a stranger. I see a paunchy, balding, superficially cheerful man who makes polite conversation, and then turns inward into himself. For a moment this pains me, and then I sigh, and just go on. If I dwelt on it I'd start feeling bitter, all the "whatever happened to the boy that I once knew" sort of feelings, the "how have we ended up politely co-existing like this?" kinds of questions would flood me. You see, it's not an unhappy life, so I can't really complain.'

It is increasingly difficult to stay together at all, let alone to stay so happily. I will consider the reasons for this in more detail in Chapter 2. Despite this well-earned silent protest at marriage, there is another side to the story. That is that not only do people still want to get married or live together for the duration, they want to be with someone they love, to be monogamous, and to stay with him or her for the rest of their lives. This belief about marriage and love has not changed.

Staying in love seems to be a concern vexing many. A mini-industry of books and studies on marriage and relationships has been spawned, in the US, in particular. Much, though not all, is inspirational or instructional. Many of the more successful books are how-to's on particular topics – such as how to capture your man and get him to marry you – or they are of an inspirational, spiritual bent (for example, the marital enrichment workshops, usually run by the Church, and the books designed to accompany them). Another mini-industry of researchers labours away at trying to isolate reasons for marital success and failure. Among others, they have found that the expression of affection, shared activities and interests, the amount of time spent together in these activities, pleasure in them, intimacy of both an emotional and physical kind, skills in negotiating and communicating are associated with successful marriages. Research has also shown that getting along with each other's families, having similar beliefs and values, and being able to find a mutually acceptable way to live with the eventual conflicts which beset any marriage are also associated with strong and happy relationships[3].

Despite all the mostly bad news about marriage, and curious as it may sound to the bulk of the jaded married population, for some people marital love is *the* transforming experience of their lives. In our current climate they are viewed as oddities. It is a strange phenomenon that, while we are supposed to feel transformed by having children, we are not supposed to be transformed by marriage. We expect to stay in love with our children forever (to think otherwise is sacrilege). But most people would say that 'being in love' recalls for them the passion of early, or secret, or thwarted relationships – they are not talking about their marriages. This leaves people like Sue whispering about their love, or pinching themselves in disbelief. Yet marriage should be a source of enormous replenishment over the years together.

That marriage, a union, a co-reliant partnership, should be transforming remains curious, because our cultural ideal of maturity exalts independence and self-reliance. The task of growing up is 'to separate and individuate', (or so say the theories), and so we expect. We are supposed to be 'launched' when grown up, our parents to suffer the 'empty nest', and when we 'leave home' we are supposed to 'break away' from the psychological grip of our families. 'Standing on your own two feet' is just that: no partner holds your hand to give you better balance. The imagery of maturity is of independence, the imagery of childhood is of dependence. To need someone, it seems to follow, is regressive. Pathological, even.

For the problem is that the relationship of the sort Sue and Mike have is actually *pathologised*: the kind of love Sue shows is seen as dependent, regressive, weak. This is particularly true for men. Women have a hard time claiming what for them may seem more natural – that is, their dependence on a relationship for a sense of nurturance, empathy and security (or, the protective functions of a relationship). They have a hard time in doing so because our dominant culture (that is, one defined chiefly by more masculine values) demeans this. So women have to deny their special knowledge about what is actually necessary for their happiness. But men are not even allowed to know and accept it about themselves in the first place. 'Dependence' is a dirty word: 'drug-dependent', 'alcohol-dependent', 'co-dependent'. Sue is strange. Happy as she is, she is embarrassed about her love. How could anyone aspire to it with impunity?

Previous books which have been successful at addressing the 'problems of modern marriage'[4] fix the 'problem' – the need for a close, loving, secure and intimate relationship – with 'therapy' which addresses the 'unfinished business' of 'old wounds' which underlie every single love relationship. This is the language of deficit and illness. And much as these books have found a ready public, for they prescribe solutions, that public will be back. The issue remains, unanswered – why do we get into relationships which have to be 'solved' through healing and therapy in the first place?

It may sound curious for someone who works as a marital therapist to object to applying the language of pathology to relationships. But it is actually through my work that I have come to conclude that the problem lies deeper than inside each individually damaged psyche. The image of millions of couples in a painful state, taking themselves off to be healed, as a solution, through help from a therapist or a spiritual experience, seems implicitly wrong. Instead, it stems from the fact that we are marginalising the need for Sue and Mike's sort of love, worshipping independence, and making that need an embarrassment. Instead of 'curing' and 'healing', the answer, as I have said, is to redefine adult love. By placing the need for protection at its centre, it makes the impulse to be in love in a protective way normal. It states that 'dependence' of that sort is deep and fulfilling, not regressive.

As I have said, it goes against current ideology to argue that it is absolutely right to expect and even demand that a relationship offer security. Current ideology has much to answer for. The theory of protective love says that your lover should be your *protector*, and as a lover you should also be protector of your loved one. We accept that the protective aspect of parent-child love is essential. Indeed, even children feel it towards their parents. In the case of children protecting parents, it comes out as fierce loyalty and, necessarily, fantasy acts of protection, rather than as real ones. Yet we are all facing the Big Bad World (which is why cartoon and fairy-tale monsters such as the Big Bad Wolf have such universal resonance, even for grown-ups), often feeling, as we do so, ridiculously like children. Just as we accept that protection is a fundamental part of parental love, we also need to admit it is fundamental to adult love.

The theory of protective love maintains that the path to enduring marital love is marked by five essential elements. In long, happy marriages each member of the couple provides for the other a sense of *protection*. Their relationship provides a consistently safe harbour. This is the quintessential element. The sense of protection in such marriages also generated additional key ingredients: the first is a couple's ability to maintain a *focus* on each other, which both demonstrates and reinforces their attention, care and loyalty; the second is their consistent demonstration of *gratitude* towards each other, which reinforces the protective sense that you are 'special' and supported by your partner; and thirdly this gratitude, protection and focus themselves engender *balance*, which also reinforces the protection because it is about mutuality of support, within the couple. Finally, the sense of *pleasure* in each other's company permeates the lives of these couples and keeps providing the glue they need to continue their mutually protective alliance.

In anticipation of the next chapter, in which I talk about the reasons why it is so difficult to maintain love, it may prove illuminating to do a simple exercise: a self-assessment of yourself and your partner. It is about your own, and what you *think* are your partner's, attitudes towards marriage. Just how central *is* your relationship in your life?

1. How do you spend your free time: more of it together, or more of it on your own?
2. Do you spend more time with your children, or with your partner on his/her own?
3. Given a choice, who would you spend your free time with: your children, your friends, on your own, or with your partner?
4. Given a choice between doing non-essential work and being with your partner, what do you characteristically choose?
5. Do you take as much trouble to please or show you care to your partner as you did in the beginning?
6. When you have an argument, or are hurt by something your partner says or does, how often do you eventually come to the notion that he or she might be as hurt, as disappointed, as vulnerable as you?

It should be obvious from your response to these questions how much attention and care you are giving to your relationship and your partner, and how much you think your partner is. But this assessment is only what you *think* your partner would score. It may, in fact, be very different, and you can only know by having your partner perform the same exercise, in reverse. How similar are your answers? How accurately did you assess each other?

11

CHAPTER TWO

Why Is It Such a Struggle to Stay in Love?

Diane, a 45-year-old doctor with two teenage children, defines love very differently from her research chemist husband, Hugh. In their first few therapy sessions, Diane spent most of the time close to tears, talking about how cold and unfeeling her husband had been for many years. 'He acts as if I don't exist. When I walk into the room and all I want to do is have a chat, tell him how my day has gone, what the children are up to, all that kind of stuff, he sits there, and reads the paper, as if I'm not even there! He doesn't love me. If he loved me he would want to listen to me, to talk to me about himself. He would want to spend time with me.' Hugh listened to this tirade with a rising sense of injustice. 'You see,' he said. 'She hates me. Love is not part of the picture. Everything I do is wrong. Other people appreciate that I'm a good, responsible husband, father, and even a friend.'

Donna, having discovered the fourth infidelity (known to her, at least) of her husband of fifteen years: 'He says he loves me, but how can he possibly love me and do this to me?' While Steve, her husband, listening with eyes brimming with tears, answers, 'I love Donna very much. I know I've hurt her, and I want to do better by her. But I've never stopped loving her.'

What do these people mean by love? Clearly not the same things. But perhaps if we ask what is the deepest function of love, we can try to synthesise some of what everyone probably means, at the most fundamental level.

In all species there is a critical period in which an infant needs to bond with its mother in order to survive[1]. The mother is not just the infant's caretaker, she is also its eyes, ears, hands and feet in the world; the baby's executor, was it were. Without the secure knowledge that the mother will act in this way, the baby cannot be assured of its continued existence. Not to put too fine a point on it, the baby *depends* on the mother for its life, and comes to enjoy a sense of security as it grows, without having to question the reliability of that dependence.

When that dependence is threatened the baby feels its existence to be threatened – alarm bells go off. In humans, babies whose primary caretakers[2] are inconsistent in their attendance to their babies' needs grow into anxious beings. Babies whose mothers continually frustrate their dependency by not responding become unattached, disengaged with others as they grow. But babies whose primary caretakers do respond, on the whole, consistently and reliably develop with security and rely on that attachment. The baby is entirely focused on its mother for its own survival and protection, and the mother needs to be focused to a large extent on the child, for the baby's dependency needs to be successfully communicated to her on the one hand, and fulfilled by her on the other.

This attachment between mother and child is a deeply experienced relationship; its meaning is attached to a sense of life itself. And so the seeds of all future relationships are contained in it. Clearly, the sense of love, which is what we can call this momentous first attachment, is necessary to the continuance of life. A deeper function for love could not be imagined.

'I thought that I was going to die when Daniel told me he was leaving me. I mean literally going to die – I could not breathe. The pain was as sharp as if he had knifed me. I thought as much about Daniel as I did about myself – he was embedded in my life, my brain, my habits; I was "Mrs Kennedy". How was I supposed to survive?'

Joy Kennedy is using the language of survival, of life and death here, as she recounts the ending of her 22-year marriage. She is talking about her sense of need for her loving relationship. She is not a baby, actually dependent on her mother to feed her and give her a roof over her head. But she feels as if she is. As she says, she thought she was 'going to die' at the prospect of being deprived of her marriage.

Yet, despite this intense need for protective love, it is difficult to cultivate marital love past the honeymoon years. It has become so because marriages are beset by internal pressures. Among the most important are:

1. Firstly, while maturity calls for independence and autonomy, the romantic ideal of love is defined by unity and merging, 'two hearts beating as one'[3]. People cite 'being best friends', 'intimacy', and attributes of self-disclosure as the most important ingredients of marriage[4]. 'I can tell her anything', is the supposed mark of a good relationship. Love as currently constructed means sharing; autonomy hardly gets a look in. Yet two grown-ups are meant to be independent and autonomous. This is an internal contradiction of the highest order for love between mature adults.

'When at sixteen I first fell in love, I wanted to be with my boyfriend all the time. Probably because we lived in different towns, our relationship lasted longer than it would have if we lived near each other; I think I would have smothered him otherwise. I dreamed of us being married and never being parted. At that time I had wanted to be a journalist, but I decided I couldn't do that, because I'd have

15

to go off on assignments, and I couldn't have borne to be apart, in my dreams, from my husband. So I gave up that idea. Even though I went on to train (to be a doctor) and to be a self-supporting, independent woman, I never really lost that ideal, of being in my lover's presence all the time. When I finally got married, at 27, it was to someone who really needs to be on his own quite a bit. He is a very successful academic, who's always going off to conferences. He's sometimes gone for a month at a time, with all his collaborations and such. When I met him I turned against the ideal of so much togetherness because he made me feel I was weedy for wanting it. I don't feel I have really got the balance right yet. I think I have taken on John's disapproval of my dependence, like I feel guilty for trapping him under false pretences, since he thought when he met me I was a paragon of independence and professionalism. I've found that I can be on my own; I've become really pretty self-reliant. But I still feel left out when he goes off. It still feels like he's leaving me, and I still disapprove of myself for feeling that.'

Joanna is a 35-year-old doctor, soon to become a mother. She is talking amiably over coffee in her kitchen, but as she confesses to her feelings of abandonment her eyes fill up. A few days earlier, her husband John had also spoken about his marriage.

'I was sent away to boarding school when I was eight. I hardly knew my father – he was a cold and punitive figure, desperately unhappy, who had no idea what to do with kids, so he had us all sent away. He and my mother were very unhappy together. He died when I was twelve, and my mother remarried a few years later. She's not very happy with this one, either. So you see, I didn't have a very good view of marriage. When I met Joanna I was bowled over by her warmth. But I was also afraid of how much she seemed to need me. I was surprised, since she was a doctor. I thought she was very independent. It turned out she wasn't. But she was willing to become less clingy, and that helped me a lot in letting myself love her. I do go off a lot, and I know she's a little jealous of my leaving, but I couldn't do my work if I felt she couldn't cope with that. If that happened we'd end up with a rotten marriage, because I'd resent her. However, I have to admit that I surprised myself last summer, when she was asked to give a paper in Honolulu. I felt a real twinge – like, how was I going to get along on my own, and how come I couldn't go, too? And when she went I really did miss her. I felt very confused – I don't really want to accept that love means being so tied to each other you can't have some independence without pain.'

2. Secondly, there is a large gender gap. Women are socialised to be creatures who live primarily through relationships. Automatically schooled in skills of disclosure, of focusing on emotions, of reading others for their unuttered needs, they get a large measure of their self-esteem and enjoyment from the web of relationships they engage in throughout their lives[5]. This is in contrast to men, whose socialisation downplays these skills, yielding other sources from which they derive most of their self-esteem: the classic 'which is more important, work or love?' divide between men and women. Men are not particularly adept confidants, or shoulders to cry on, but they find women who are. Most men cite a woman as their main confidante, but, then, so do women. And men do not cite their relationships as their main source of self-esteem, while women invariably do[6]. This yields a situation in which relationships are sources of most esteem for women, and women, still less powerful in the wider scheme of things than men, do not define what is most valued in the world.

Nicola, a 40-year-old mother of three, married for fifteen years, talks about the turning point in her life, the time when she discovered that her adored husband had had an affair seven years earlier, with a close mutual friend. This discovery plunged her into a depression, the focus of which was how worthless she was. Over their years together Nicola had been reluctant to attend social functions, since she dreaded being asked the question: 'And what do you do?' She didn't 'do' anything she could point to, apart from raise her family brilliantly and happily, volunteer at her children's school, and help out in her husband's private medical practice. During the early child-rearing years it was easy to avoid nagging self-doubts about her worth: too tired for much socialising, they rarely went out. But she was aware that she felt threatened by what she dubbed the 'power suiters' – women she imagined were out conquering the world like men. Her husband had a few women friends, mostly doctors with whom he worked. Nicola avoided them as much as possible, but one made determined overtures to her, and slowly they became friends. The slight edge of threat and jealousy of this woman's apparent easy independence and achievement never quite left Nicola, and when she found out that this was the woman with whom her husband had had an affair, her self-esteem plummeted further. She could not see herself as anything but a sordid failure next to a woman who 'had it all'.

But her husband, Martin, says he was baffled, that he doesn't know what drove him into an affair, because what continues to fascinate him about Nicola is '. . . her energy and efficiency and her gift with people'. 'I have never felt she was less of a person than any of the women I have worked with,' he protests, still unsure of why he had the affair, beyond the bland explanation of a 'mid-life crisis'. Unconvinced that it would not happen again, Nicola announced she and the children were leaving. This produced not rage, but depression in Martin, who stopped working and began consuming large doses of anti-depressants. 'I could not bear to be without her. I phoned her every few hours, to check that she was still there (at her mother's house). I wanted to talk to her for hours on end. She showed the most incredible patience listening to me going on and on about my guilt and mid-life crisis. It is to her immense credit as a woman with backbone that she stayed despite what I did. I don't know if I could have done the same,' Martin reports.

Nevertheless, as a result of discovering the affair, Nicola needed an explanation so that she could be secure Martin would not have another affair. Comparing herself to his lover, she found an explanation in: 'I wasn't interesting and independent enough'. As a result of the affair, Nicola enrolled as a mature student and is about to be articled as a solicitor. She thinks she will do family law, 'a fitting specialty'.

The shakiness of the state of relationships today may be largely a function of the fact that men do not value them as much as they value their achievements at work; as long as relationships are a 'woman's thing', they will get short shrift in the world. Work hours will increase, families will continue to be divided by work rather than supported by it, and fathers will continue to be on the sidelines of child-rearing within families.

Tony and Anne bought an old house when they moved with their two tiny children to take up jobs at a market research company. The house needed a lot of work, which they could not afford to contract out. So, during their children's first five and seven years of life, respectively, this couple went to work, repaired the house, looked after children and did little else. Then Tony was promoted, which meant taking a job at head office, a 45-minute commute away. It also meant later meetings, and more travelling, to oversee other sites. It fell to Anne to organise the children's childcare, to attend school functions, to run the domestic side of their lives. But Anne had also been on the fast track. A promotion was in the offing for her, as well. When it came up she turned it down, which was fine for the children, but in some ways terrible for Tony, as Anne's resentment of him began to rocket. 'What was I supposed to do? Give the kids a key and say "have a good life?" I had no choice, but I don't know why he thought he did. While we were spending all those years doing up this house and living on little money and less sleep, I kept thinking "this will be over soon and we'll get back to having fun together, to being good friends and enjoying life together again". But he obviously wasn't thinking that way: he took the first chance to opt out, to work more. We hardly know him any more.'

Closely related to this is the fact that our cultural institutions do not support the kind of interdependent marriage I am lobbying for in this book. The fact that they promote independence and autonomy instead is probably a result of the historical fact that the extended family living together is largely now a thing of the past; couples are expected to live away from their own families (sometimes hundreds and thousands of miles) in order to work and support the new families they create. They *have* to be independent of their old ties and supports.

Whereas in the past the desire for friendship, daily conversation and favours from your friends and family was not seen as needy, nor necessarily evidence of a failing, today to live a life centred around friends and family appears stunted, or undeveloped. To appear needy for love and friendship is often seen as an embarrassment. This is true to the extent that now, with women and men usually both working, these days (the number of women remaining at home throughout their children's lives is minuscule) even within the nuclear family jobs often keep couples apart. Sometimes this can mean actually living apart. This in itself can often spell the end of a particular marriage.

Leah and William married when William was finishing his PhD. and Leah starting her first job as an editor. She was also pregnant with their only child, who is now nine. For the first year of their son's life William was home, writing up his thesis and applying for jobs. That is the single year of their marriage which both report as happy. William then took a teaching job at a university two hours away. He spent two nights of the week in a flat near his job, rushing home as soon as his last class or meeting ended. Then Leah was head-hunted by another publisher for a much better, higher-paying job. Her new office was further away, adding an additional hour to the daily journey. Sometimes William had to stay over an extra night or two since the drive was now so long and difficult. As he became more successful, invitations to speak and consult came in from all over the world. Sometimes he would be gone for weeks at a time. Finally, Leah learned to make and unmake plans around William, disbelieving his promises about coming home after untold disappointments. She began to behave like a single parent. She stopped showing him their son's school letters, and stopped consulting him about their son's problems. When she stopped showing him their son's school reports William's anger exploded. At this point, years of pent-up rage came spewing out of both of them. Their physical separation had become an emotional one.

This story illustrates the fall-out from the fact that there are so few institutional supports for putting relationships first, for being a truly interdependent couple. For this couple to have made such a choice would have meant one 'sacrificing my career'. Women used to do this; now, even women can no longer be seen to be making such choices.

3. Thirdly, after the fairy-tale courtship and wedding, a dangerous silence settles around marriage. This is demonstrated in the confounding of marital happiness with familial happiness. 'One big, happy family' includes the couple, at its centre, of course, but there is very little understanding of how that couple can be happy or unhappy together apart from the family as a whole. Families are meant to share togetherness: Sunday worship, family holidays, weekend shared activities. Outside of sex, there are few spheres preserved solely for the couple. Couples

who go off on holiday without the children think twice, and not just because it is hard to get childcare. They get smirks – 'Oh, off for a dirty weekend, are you?' – as if sex is the only possible reason they could have for slicing off a chunk from family or individual time. Couple pleasure and happiness, as apart from family, is deeply undervalued.

Chris and Tim are the envy of their friends. They have been married for 21 years, and still celebrate Valentine's Day as if it were Christmas. They are both immensely witty and energetic and clearly delight in each other, giving their friends tremendous pleasure in their repartee. Each matches the other in their capacity for enjoyment – of wine, food, music and conversation. They are clearly still in love. There is one chink in the armour: their teenage daughter Jane, who feels excluded.

Tim and Chris belong to a sailing club. When Jane was younger she was brought along, eventually crewing for them. It seemed a family pursuit, but at thirteen Jane withdrew. What sparked the friction between them was a major change in Jane's social life: her two best friends had moved away and she had changed schools. Feeling friendless, she became withdrawn, moody and demanding. She resented her parents' pleasure in each other and quailed at the thought of large social gatherings. Hence her refusal to join them at the club. While understanding and indulging her need for their reassurance and company, Chris and Tim drew the line at sailing. But they had not reckoned on Jane's wild tantrums. Every weekend, just before they left, Jane tried to sabotage their departure, hysterically threatening to harm herself. Usually this worked: as the hours of trying to reason with her ticked by, whether or not to sail became a moot point. Chris and Tim found themselves in the unfamiliar state of persistent bickering and ill will.

When they realised what was happening they decided that Jane would no longer undermine their pleasure in each other;

at the next opportunity they would sail again. It happened that the next week they were entered for a long race, which entailed staying the night. They made arrangements for Chris's mother to stay with Jane. And, of course, on the day of departure Jane came down with a stomach ailment which, however, did not have the desired effect of preventing their departure. Leaving a contact number, medical information and other helpful hints and contacts for Chris's mother, they left, with trepidation which faded as soon as they relaxed into the weekend. Behind them they left a despondent young girl hurling accusations of their selfishness. While this was difficult to bear, they were in for a shock on their return. For by then Chris's mother had joined her granddaughter in bitter criticism, attacking her daughter and son-in-law as selfish and irresponsible. Baffled and hurt, feeling unfairly judged for having put their marriage first, Chris and Tim wonder whether pleasure in each other must be submerged at all costs and all times if a demand arises first from the wider family.

The silence about the couple within the family stems from the insidious idea that the romance which set off the courtship remains the sparkplug of the relationship. As a consequence of this kind of blinded thinking, relationships, including marriage, have come to be measured in the same way: 'how good does it make me feel?' This has been dubbed the 'pure relationship'[7] and can be a pernicious force.

The importance of romance, especially when combined with our current companionate, egalitarian model of marriage ('best friend', at least lip service to being 'equal' in terms of power) has conspired to make the sense of being in something ideal, even heroic (in a romantic sense) together the only important motivation for staying together. The companionate marriage is one which demands talking, disclosure, sharing and feeling good together. It is also detached from the wider family network. Once such a detachment occurs so does a lessening in interests and concerns outside of the nuclear unit. Detached from the frame of a wider social network, it can be 'pure' – functioning only to make its participants feel good. The resulting romantic 'tale' of companionate marriage is that of an intensely shared, *private* life between the two protagonists. Feeling good about that sharing and the quality of that sharing between the two becomes the only significant measure of whether the romance, or the romantic tale of the marriage, is being achieved.

This leads to a real problem. Whether a relationship works or not (that is, whether it feels good in an intimate, sharing way) is the main criterion for its continued existence. It is no wonder then that our modern relationships are so unstable. Much of the time they fail to measure up. Much of the time they are under siege, fallen victim to normal and abnormal stressors, and much of the time, even happy couples experience periods of being disgruntled with the quality of their relationships.

This sort of detached, romantic model contributes to the silence around what is the reality of modern marriage: the day-to-day rubbing along together, the continuous need for delicate negotiations. This is a reality which demands work, in the same way work relationships do. Domestic negotiations are, necessarily, even more delicate than work ones: both partners are especially vulnerable to each other. Negotiations need to pivot around the idea that each partner needs and wants protection from the other, as much as around the desire to win the stated objective over which they are negotiating. Chapter 4 will discuss this sort of protective negotiating. But this is not the kind of thing people think they will have to learn when they take their marriage vows.

4. Fourthly, we define love in largely female terms. Success in love relationships is largely female-defined, yet it is set within a social structure which demeans the feminine, and makes it a sign of weakness to reveal vulnerability.

This point may be the most critical one. Because of it we develop women who are 'experts in relationships' who wed men who are, by definition, not. In a survey and interviews done on heterosexual American couples between 1980 and 1983, it was found that people who were either very polarised in their gender roles or who expected the 'feminine version' of love were less sanguine about their relationships[7]. In fact, 73 per cent of divorces in this country are initiated by women. Women, who define the terms of love, feeling cheated of it by men who are not as adept as they at love, are walking away from marriages.

The inability of so many men and women to interpret each other's gestures as loving and the consistent distortion of many unfamiliar behaviours as 'selfish' or beside the point are critical steps in the crumbling of relationships[8]. In the study referred to above, which looked at the different ways men and women gave and experienced love, one set of findings concerned the way men and women thought they expressed love and affection.

According to this study, men most often complain that their wives are not interested enough in sex, which for them is the expression of love, while women complain that their husbands won't listen to or talk to them, which is the way women develop intimacy and encode love. Men declare that they are, indeed, providing help, practical support and the labour to provide the material necessities and luxuries to support family life. This they also label as expressing love. In response, they say that their wives fail to appreciate this. Instead, they assert that, like a slap in the face, their wives nag them to come home earlier, clearly not appreciating that they work so long and hard in large part because this is the way they show love.

For their parts, wives complain that these same husbands pay little heed to the myriad ways in which they continuously nourish them. Wives' caring is demonstrated through different gestures – through stocking up on soap and toothpaste, through making dental appointments, through shopping for them and cooking their meals, through managing their social lives, through sharing the minutiae of their days in order to feel close, and finally and most decidedly, through then talking to them about what many of these husbands consider the trivia of their lives. In loving couples, such respective gestures do not go unheeded; they are understood as the constant and continuing expression of love, as expressive of it as gift-wrapped roses or sonnets.

Donald and Katherine have been married for eight years. Katherine complains that Donald has never made her feel special. Donald does not understand. 'I offered to take her to Switzerland, to Tenerife, to Paris,' he explains. 'She should have known that that meant I thought she was special. I wouldn't just go with anybody or on my own. Those are special places, and they cost a lot of money to get to, so I would have had to work hard to get us there, so she would have to be a special person for me to make that effort and take her with me.' But Katherine interpreted his offers as, 'He wanted to go, but needed a companion, for which, as wife, I'm the logical choice.' She complains that she does not think Donald thinks she's special, because he '. . . doesn't tell me he's proud of me, he never compliments me, and he never buys me presents. I buy my own birthday presents and I give them to him to wrap them up.'

5. Fifthly, there is the problem of the gender divide. Men and women both want to love and to be loved, but their very gender is often what divides them. A man's experience is very different from a woman's. 'What do women want?' posed a baffled Freud, the man. 'All men are rapists,' claims an angry Andrea Dworkin, the woman. Threaded throughout relationships is this importance of gender. It is *as* men and women that adjustments to each other are made. Individual requirements for love are forged by early experiences in the family, but these

are forged around the fact of gender. How do men and women manage not just to *want* to love each other, but how do men read the needs of their women, how do women grasp the needs of their men, and how do both end up doing what the other needs? It is indeed difficult to cross this gender divide.

In consequence of both these gender differences and the debasement of female values, even though we expect them to drive relationships, heterosexual relationships in particular are in deep trouble. It may be helpful to pause here and, as a means of personalising these points about men and women, try a self-assessment of yourself and your partner, and your attitudes about what constitutes loving behaviour.

Here are some ways men say they demonstrate love. Think about how important *you* think they are as expressions of love. Then, in the same way, think about how *you think your partner* would rate the same statements:

1. I'm a good provider.
2. I fix things around the house.
3. I look after the car, making sure it's safe to drive.
4. I take her out to nice places.
5. I want to make love to her frequently.
6. I look after her safety whenever it's in doubt.
7. I help out with technical, practical tasks and suggestions.

Now here are some ways women say they demonstrate love. Think about these statements in the same fashion as you did the first set, above:

1. I tell him about my day.
2. I tell him about my feelings.
3. I ask him about his day and his feelings.
4. I try to get him to talk to me if I think he isn't feeling quite right.

5. I look after, or am responsible for, the smooth daily running of his home.
6. I look after our joint social life.
7. I bring issues up so that we can address our problems.

How well do your assessments and those of your partner match up? Is there a gender divide within you as a couple in your beliefs about what constitutes loving behaviour? (It would not be unusual if there were, or if both of you actually valued the women's statements more than the men's.) It would not be surprising to find that there was room for you as a couple to become more clear about what efforts, exactly, are being made, by whom, on behalf of the relationship; it would not be surprising if each of you was not recognising at least some of your partner's efforts.

In consequence of all of the above points, we are left struggling with ideas of marital love rife with contradictions. It is difficult to 'perform' marital love. Gender and sex are not the same. Because gender is socially constructed it is, consequentially, 'performed': we learn exactly what to do as women and as men, and this includes how we perform love as women and as men. Couples can indeed 'perform' love in enduring marriages but only if they are guided by two facts: first, each acknowledges the importance of their own and the other's deep interdependence, and, second, they then screen the other's 'performance' of love through this lens. In other words, women have to interpret or decode men's loving gestures and actions, which are undeniably different from the ones they make as women; and men have to do the same in reverse.

Love and therapy: getting the love we need

When people are questioned about what they most want in a partner, they say 'Someone who will be my best friend', 'someone I can talk to', 'someone I can tell anything to', 'someone who understands me'. These are qualities of intimacy and attachment. Men and women both rank these sorts of qualities most highly. More men than women report high levels of satisfaction in their marriages, and more men have wives to whom they can talk, disclose and who make efforts to understand them than women have husbands. This is of course no accident. The view that marriage be based on a love founded in intimacy, which is fostered by the talking and relational skills bred commonly in women, is a very feminine view of love, as we have seen[9]. But the equation of talk and intimacy and attachment has become almost a kneejerk one, and dangerous.

As a result of this association, marital therapy is usually focused on getting couples to learn to talk to each other more, to share more time and activities together, and to disclose more to each other. Much of this is essential. We shall see in Chapter 5, which looks at Focus, as well as throughout the discussion of all the five factors, that clear and direct communication as well as giving enough time and energy to your partner are essential mechanisms for putting the factors in operation. However, much is also misguided.

The main thrust of such therapy puts the onus on couples to pursue a kind of ideal of love in which two people 'merge'. Intimacy, especially in terms of time, interests and talking together a great deal, is emphasised. It promotes this feminised way of loving, and thereby leaves out the sorts of loving acts which men perform well. It also avoids the question of how we would ever get men to achieve this ideal – the talking at great length, the sharing of vulnerabilities with frequency, the expression of love through words and romantic gestures, for instance. We end up with a lopsided expertise (women only) and also with a devaluation of other gestures of love, such as the instrumental ones, which also provide nurturance and protection, which draw on men's expertise.

However, as we have already seen, in urging this it also

contradicts other prevailing cultural messages, those which exalt individualism, those which, as we have said, devalue the expression of vulnerability and dependence on another. The tradition of therapy which aims for 'separation and individuation' in these ways can actually be unhelpful, fuelling dissatisfactions and disregarding ways couples can strengthen what they already have going for them but have overlooked. This is not to say that marital therapy is unhelpful, because it can obviously save marriages. But the aims and recommendations of the sessions should be looked at critically, or couples will keep landing back in the same minefields.

Instead, couples can largely help themselves most in the first instance by refocusing their view of healthy love. In the second, they need to be prepared to become very *self-conscious and reflective about themselves* as actors within their relationships. They need to make a lot of their choices about how to respond to their partner's *unspontaneous* and *self-conscious*. In this way, their experiences of each other will change, so that resentment and defensiveness will be replaced with openness and generosity. In time, in part because these new, pleasant experiences are rewarding, the old habits of defensiveness which produce a downward spiral (of resentment and alienation) are replaced by new ones, which produce an upward spiral (of affection, and reciprocally protective behaviour).

Couples need to become reflective about these things:

1. What does my partner really need or what is he/she really trying to say (what is the emotional point), given that he or she is actually in essence a vulnerable, dependent person?
2. What is the effect on my partner of my actions, given that he/she is essentially a vulnerable, dependent person?
3. Couples need to be prepared to establish ground rules (see Chapter 11) for treating each other delicately and to

discard notions that they can second-guess their partners, because usually that means they have made the other into something invulnerable.

CHAPTER THREE

Protection: the Safe Harbour of Love

'When my parents took me to boarding school when I was thirteen, I put on a very brave face. Actually, it didn't take much effort at first because I was really very excited. But then the moment of their departure came. My face crumpled and suddenly I was in tears. Moments earlier I'd been as cocky as could be, thinking this wonderful new world was all mine. I truly shocked myself. It took me weeks to get adjusted. At nights I just cried myself to sleep, trying desperately not to let the other boys see or hear me.'

Graham is now a 54-year-old father of four. He is having very similar feelings now as he lets go of his last child, who is off to university. But Graham is a widower. He had no one with whom to share his pain at bidding his child farewell, and this causes him almost as much grief as both the memories of that earlier separation and this present, impending one.

Mothers and fathers, through their loving care, protect their children through the normally occurring disruptions of growing up. But life lived in this way never stops, since grown-up life itself offers an unfolding series of disruptions to all lives. What does stop is having parents to ease the way or to help you through it. As grown-ups, too, we feel we need protection or allies to help us combat the effects of disruptions or traumas. Why should we not?

It is essentially crazy to deny this. Yet this is what we are asked to do as adults, as we have said in Chapter 1: we grow up in order to separate, be launched, to individuate and to move on. But, in fact, the world is, if anything, harder and harsher when we are grown-ups: real threat – of death, illness, destitution, defeat – confronts us rather more directly. Don't societies rely on armies – that is, associations of people, alliances – to fend off attacks on societal levels? Yet the language of partnership, and alliance, of mutual protection, vanishes when we speak of normal, which means difficult, adult life. The impulse to be in an alliance with someone, which helps and protects you through life, to expect that that is what constitutes love, does not vanish. It goes underground. It becomes labelled 'regressive'. It belongs to childhood, and to pathology.

The other idea of adult development emphasises, rather than marginalises, the adult's need for a relationship, and redefines psychological maturity. In it the Iron Man, who is an island, the John Wayne icon of adult maturity, retires to the world of mythology.

This dominant model of healthy adult development has promoted both the silence about marriage after the wedding and the emphasis on reliable, nurturing love during childhood but not adulthood. What 'separation and individuation' implies is that the process of growing up is a process of gradually defining yourself apart from your parents, becoming 'independent' and growing away from them. When you are truly mature you are 'self-supporting', 'autonomous', and 'able to function on your own'[1]. While there is truth in this, it is only a partial truth. Taking this model of maturity literally can lead to disease and instability[2]. For it ignores the necessity for dependence: it glosses over the fact that being in relationships is as important and healthy as breathing. It leaves out the need for a mutually dependent, safe relationship. That sort of relationship has indeed been linked in studies to mental and physical health. People who are in good marriages or marriage-like relationships are less likely to fall ill, on the whole have better mental health and live longer. Not to put too fine a point on it, it seems that such relationships are central to survival.

When Mark, a 38-year-old father of two, whom we shall meet in Chapter 8, lost his job a few years ago, he, like many others who face unemployment, began to sink into depression. His wife, Margaret, says that she would leave to take their children to school or go out to do some shopping, and when she would get home she would find him 'still sitting in that same chair, still staring straight ahead, as if he hadn't even moved. He didn't want to get up to do anything.' This went on for a few weeks. Margaret tells about this time and how her sense of protectiveness towards her husband, her efforts to help him out of his vulnerable and painful state, paid off:

'I would say to him that things would get better, because when you hit rock bottom you can only go back up, you can't go any further down, you know. And of course he didn't believe me, when I said things like this. But it just gradually got through to him . . . we just talked and talked and talked.' Finally, through her persistence and through Mark's response to her caring, it worked.

Mark corroborates this: 'I went through a period about four and a half or five years ago where I'd lost my job and I didn't know whether I was going to be able to work again, based on the fact that there weren't that many jobs available . . . In a nutshell, Margaret said, "Don't be silly, you've got to fight. We'll support you as much as we can, but there's something out there," and slowly something clicked in my head and said, "Oh, well, I am being silly. I am being stupid. I must fight back . . . to be able to support my family." ' In this case it was Margaret's constant 'talking and talking and talking' to him which finally reached him, first, and second, the responsibility which he bore to others, those in his family ('I must fight back . . . to support my family') which motivated him out of his depression.

Because she tuned into his vulnerability, while hers was pushed aside (for, of course, as Mark was the main bread-winner, Margaret and her children themselves were vulnerable when Mark lost his job), Margaret was not going to stand by and let this continue. 'You can't stand by and let someone you love just sink into that kind of state . . . We all needed him.' So she kept telling him this, that they needed him, that things would get better, that she believed in him, and that she needed him to believe that things would get better, too. At first he couldn't listen to her, the words just floating past him. Slowly she began to make sense. As his wife and children are '. . . the most important things to me', he 'couldn't let them down. Slowly I began to listen and believe Margaret.' And within a matter of a few weeks Mark was back among the living, and eventually found a job, partly, he reports, because of his positive attitude.

A model of maturity which focuses on emotional connections and relationships should replace the old one. It frees us to concentrate on the vital importance in real maturity of emphasising the various needs for others, especially when in love. When we can bring the fundamental nature of our need as grown-ups for connection and protection through alliance with another into the foreground, exalting it as evolved and mature, we can move towards accepting it in ourselves and our lovers. We are on the first step of the path to real and lasting love.

In fact, the task has fallen to women psychologists[3] to challenge these dominant ideas. In their descriptions of women's psychological development, women's central concerns are their relationships with others. These researchers and theorists have variously found that in a series of contexts, from their reactions to rape and trauma, to their moral choices in difficult ethical situations, to making sense of their journey through adolescence and beyond, women consistently show through their reasoning how pivotal and elevated at every stage is their need for relationships. This model directly contradicts the male, macho, stiff-upper-lip, man-alone-against-nature-and-the-elements, pioneer mentality described above. It confronts the old model of object-relations and ego psychologists as a mark of adulthood. Women, these psychologists claim, are socialised to value relationships. Their psychological and moral styles of thinking have been contrasted to men's. This work has shown that in some deep ways men and women are different.

Yet not so different, after all, it turns out. When women leave men, men fall apart. Unlike women, men re-enter relationships headfirst. Men, not women, jump straight into new relationships when their old ones fall apart. Men are bereft without women. After their relationships break down, men more frequently end up in hospitals, with either physical or psychological complaints. Indeed, women tend to cope better, even finding more peace remaining single (even with children) than they did in difficult marriages[4]. Men are, it seems, very *dependent*.

Jonathan is an executive in the leisure industry. He sets up leisure clubs and sells entertainment packages to businesses. He travels quite a bit for his job. He earns well and lives well. He has always thought that if you indulge your wife, give her money for entertainment, clothes, food and luxuries she will be happy and you will have done your job. He and his wife did not spend a lot of time talking, by his own admission, because 'I really don't know how to do that. I'm not comfortable talking about my feelings. She used to complain about it, but I really thought, "I'm doing my job, aren't I? What can she complain about?" She's got a great house, great car, great holidays, we belong to a wonderful club – a great life?' One day, after four years of marriage, he returned from a business trip to Mauritius to find a note from his wife and all her possessions gone. Unable to accept her leaving, he stalked her, following her around, phoning her at all hours, demanding that she come back. Each time, of course, he was rebuffed. Her plain and simple complaint was that he had given her little time and even less conversation. So, in his absence, she had found someone who would, and had moved in with him. Persisting in his single-minded battle to bring her back, Jonathan became seriously ill, suffering from malnutrition, excessive drink and exhaustion. After two months in this attenuated state he made a suicide attempt, ending up in hospital and consequently under psychiatric care. This follow-up therapy made small dents into his life – in an overly compliant way he set about trying to make friendships, to look after himself, to try to replace his largely materialistic values with an appreciation of simpler pleasures and accomplishments, but he retained throughout a low-level depression and inertness. It was not really until he met another woman that Jonathan came back to life. Though his doctors were sceptical, Jonathan ended his treatment, for to him, this was 'cured'. And it was certainly true that he looked like 'the new man' he claimed himself to be shortly after this new relationship began.

Despite this, those same vulnerable men have been denied the right to acknowledge the central importance of relationships in their lives. Manly Tarzan, strong in his solitude, is the apotheosis of male maturity. As a number of people have claimed[5], compared to women, men have literally lacked the language for the need for connection and psychological refuge. Instead, when grieving, they have been forced to act out their feelings, against themselves, by falling ill, for instance, or else, in perhaps hasty acts of attempted salvation (with a strong theme of denial) by forming quick new liaisons. Yet, given this weight of evidence, even though it apparently bears little relation to reality, the male model of maturity remains our dominant story of how to become a mature adult. It has muscled out the apparently truer female one – truer because it emphasises the central importance of relationships.

Jim's story illustrates this. Jim is a 50-year-old ex-executive. After being fired from a prestigious director's position for gross alcohol abuse and breaches of company policy about alcohol consumption at work, his GP referred him for psychotherapy. His symptoms were described as agitated depression with frequent outbursts of anger and uncontrolled drinking. Behind this façade lay the real emotional story, of a marriage in its final days. The marital breakdown had been precipitated by his son's surgery for a potential cancer; at the hour of his family's deepest need, Jim went on a bender and vanished from sight. Discovered by his brother, drunk, miles away, he confessed that his child's confrontation with mortality had brought unbearable nightmares of his own mother's death when he was eight, a death which had gone almost virtually unremarked in his life. He had been at boarding school when told of his mother's completely unexpected death from an embolism, by his housemaster. His father had decided Jim was too young to attend a funeral, and that it would, in addition, be too disruptive of his education to take him out of school in the middle of term. No one at his school comforted him nor filled in important details for him; he was entirely excluded from even the restricted form of mourning the rest of his family was afforded. On his return home at the holidays, his remote and formal father did not mention his mother, although her effects still dotted the house. And when his father remarried a few years later, Jim felt it would have been disrespectful to his stepmother to mention his mother in front of either parent. He seemed, even from this early age, to become apparently self-sufficient and he never looked back. Yet the complaint his wife had lodged throughout their married life was that he was cold, unfeeling and rejecting. Throughout their marriage she had turned unhappily to others at times of emotional need, even toying with affairs from time to time. After Jim's crucial disappearance she decided to leave him, as her son's bout with death sharpened her own sense of deprivation. One year on, Jim's wife reported how much happier she was on her own, while Jim was still struggling, unable to accept the separation.

John, a 53-year-old father of one daughter, who has been with Nina, 44, for sixteen years (and who we will meet again in detail in Chapter 5) tells a story in marked contrast. When he and Nina met, he owned two very successful nightclubs which took a lot of time and energy, as successful businesses do. Nina was a flight attendant, who had trained as an artist. In the early days of their relationship the fact that they were not together all the time was not a problem. But then Nina became pregnant. This brought about a testing crisis, the death of their first child (Nina had become pregnant before they were married, before they were explicitly committed to each other). At five and a half months Nina went into labour, gave birth and lost the baby, who had survived for just over one day. John talks about his vigil at the hospital, his dashing back to the clubs, for which he had major responsibility and so could not neglect, only to turn around and dash back to Nina at the hospital, and then afterwards at home, where she was convalescing. John tells of the events which eventually all together led to his changed priorities, his focus on his relationship with Nina and his defocusing on his business career.

'I had to be strong for Nina. The hardest thing I have ever had to do was to tell my wife our baby had died. Being strong for her helped me, in a sense, because I had to mask my emotions . . . When Nina came home from the hospital we talked about a great many things and found comfort in each other . . . It was a very sharp welding together of a lot of things that maybe we had thought about in the previous couple of years, but never found the time or the correct time, the proper opportunity, to talk about . . . many important things. Prior to that, I was keeping back a lot of things, not necessarily intentionally, a number of secrets you could call them. As we got to know each other better these got whittled down . . . It got to the point where I totally trusted Nina, totally trusted her.'

After a short while, Nina became pregnant again, and went into premature labour at exactly the same point in the pregnancy. This time, after a traumatic labour and delivery, the baby survived, only to enter a prolonged period of desperate health problems, with her survival very much in question. In the end their daughter survived but with very damaged sight. John again was in the position of dashing back and forth.

'(Finally) it was in 1991 – that was the watershed I'd been building up to for about six or eight months. It was either the nightclubs went or . . . my health was getting worse' (he had contracted ME). 'Enough was enough,' he says. 'I decided I didn't need all that stress. Nina and the little one were what was worth it.' Eventually John sold up his clubs, and retired early to the couple's idyllic spot in the countryside, where he started and now runs a charity for the partially sighted, and Nina has a studio where she paints. Now he says, 'I don't consider too may things from my own point of view. It's much more considering the family's . . . almost everything you do is with the consideration of "well, will that fit in with what Nina's doing?" '

Protection as the basis for love: attachment theory

The need for protection as the basis of love has been postulated by attachment theory. In this theory of development, a baby is seen to form an attachment (the basis of love) with its mother (or other primary caretaker), who is essentially its protector – she feeds, clothes and responds to it; she is the executor of its needs. It relies on her for its very survival, and when that reliance is secure and predictable it begins to form a secure attachment to her, the basis of a secure love.

When it is unreliable, or alternatively when it is depriving or punitive, the relationship is suffused with insecurity and anxiety, on the one hand, or denial, depression and the inability to engage, on the other [6].

The first relationship is the progenitor of all relationships, the template upon which they are formed. Attachment theory puts it that to form such relationships is instinctive. Species other than humans show the mechanisms for developing attachment relationships between the young and their protectors. In a Nobel prize-winning piece of research, Konrad Lorenz showed that these mechanisms are inborn to the extent that when you take a newborn goose away from her mother she will 'imprint' on a human who steps into the mother's protective role; the baby goose will behave to that human as if he is the mother. The baby goose in that sense 'loves' the human 'mother'. In this way, 'love' is very close to the baby's knowing that it will be protected.

The past model of healthy adult development has explained the normal time of 'adolescent rebellion', when teenagers, in particular, seem to turn against their parents (or at the very least begin to de-idealise them) as a necessary growing up and out phase. But in the new model of development this can be seen quite differently: the need to make other attachments is what characterises this time, as well. A large part of the focus of young adult lives is the question of who will replace the parents, who now will take centre stage in the drama of the heart? The drive to make more attachments is more of the same of what we see in babies, in their mothers – in fact, all through life. It may even be that one reason so many early marriages fail is that the former attachment (to the parents) is still too central; there isn't yet enough room to give the new one pride of place.

More recently, studies of adult love relationships have charted the similarity between the behaviour of lovers, especially early in their relationships, and that between mother and baby[7] for instance, the function of the relationship being above all, to provide protection, security and consistency.

The anxiety which arises in the early stages of love between adults – for example, should the lover not return; or if he/she does not reassure you that he/she loves you; the intensity of the need to be in the lover's presence – these are qualities which mark both relationships. The search for a secure attachment seems to underlie both. In other words, from these studies of human attachment needs and behaviours it appears that the need for security, for safety, to be able to rely upon the beneficence and support of your lover (all of which are in a large sense about feeling protected through love) underlie human psychology. The need for this sense of protection is at the base of all love relationships. Then, when marriage enters, as some good recent research asserts[8], its assumed reliability and consistency provide a context for this protective function.

Terry and Gigi met when they were sixteen. Gigi's parents were born in China, but Gigi was born in Leeds. She has always considered herself British first. She has excelled in school, and socialised primarily with British-born friends. Her parents, however, have maintained their Chinese customs and attitudes and discouraged her from academic achievements, instead wanting her to work in the family business until she met a suitable Chinese husband. She and Terry met at a debating match. Terry comes from a large family in which he has felt odd – the serious one. The two felt as if they found each other. Her parents knew nothing of Terry's existence for months, until a neighbour made a casual reference to seeing the two together. Gigi was duly forbidden to see Terry; her response was to move in with him, which is where she stayed until both finished school. They now share a flat which they own. Terry is putting her through university and she plans to do the same for him when she graduates. They have been together for nine years.

'I never felt understood or supported by my parents. I feel

very unhappy about the way they have treated me,' says Gigi. 'They took good care of me when I was very young, and wanted the best for me, but they truly abandoned me when I grew up differently from them. I was a very lonely person when I met Terry, and he gave, and still gives, me all the support and confidence in the world. He truly supports me, believes in me, tolerates my bad points. He would never leave me or let me down. He understands me. He was the first person who ever did and probably still is the only person who really does. We are a real partnership which survives against the odds.' Terry adds, 'Gigi had a really rough time and I would like to make up for that and give her the happiness that was lacking. In return she understands me. I'm a complex personality. She gives me confidence and encouragement. I like my responsibilities towards her. They feel right.'

Terry and Gigi have found each other; the hunger for acceptance and understanding was so enormous that Terry's love for her fitted her like a glove; it triumphed over her past experience of being misunderstood by her own parents. Her admiration of and gratitude to him filled his hunger to be accepted instead of being shunned as 'odd'. Out of these deep vulnerabilities has grown a strength in a relationship constructed to protect each person in it.

What the protective function of love looks like – what it is

Protection between lovers has the following qualities:

1. You feel (i.e., you emphathise with) your partner's vulnerability. Especially at the courtship stage, most couples have no difficulty with this. Typically, they are very concerned not to hurt the other's feelings; they notice even infinitesimal signs indicating that something they have done or said has been painful to their partner.

It is part of what so strongly connects lovers early on; it springs from a feeling that you share a set of nerve endings and responses to the world. One person's pain is the other's. (As Terry says: 'Gigi had such a rough time – I wanted to give her the happiness that was lacking.')

2. You feel that your partner feels as alone or unique in the world as you yourself sometimes do, when you yearn for a secure alliance. John says of Nina, when he talks of their shared life with their cherished partially-sighted daughter: 'You know exactly what the other has been through. We understand each other perfectly.' Or, as Gigi says of Terry: 'He believes in me; he tells me I can do whatever I want to. Terry understands me; we're a pair – I can't imagine myself without him.' Again, this is an experience which is part of what helps form a deep connection at the early stages of relationships: partners recognise each other across the proverbially crowded room, or planet, and rush to their proverbial sides. Hence, each is not alone.

3. You bear witness to the specialness of your partner's feelings. These can be either pleasurable or painful ones. John says, with tears in his eyes, even though it is now thirteen years on: 'There has never been a more painful moment in my life than the one when I had to tell my wife that our baby had died.' This was the most painful moment, not the one when he himself learned of his baby's death. This is most marked in times of especial sadness or joy (births, deaths, major transitions) but it also can be present over small but meaningful events (such as when your partner is praised over a report or upset by criticism at work). John says, 'I was really proud of Nina's papers – I typed them up – when she was doing her art history course at college. I really learned something from them, too.'

Protection in happy partnerships gets played out in the following ways:

1. When you recognise your partner's vulnerability (for instance his or her insecurity, pain, anxiety, fear, doubt, or disappointment; this can occur either when you are told about it or when you recognise or intuit it from other more inchoate signs), and in recognising it, you:

    a. physically comfort him/her (e.g., put your arms around your partner, hug, stroke, or hold his/her hand).

    b. say comforting or supportive things to him/her.

    c. offer constructive and supportive advice.

    d. listen empathically (as shown by nodding, making eye contact, giving assuring sounds of acknowledgement; giving prompts to go on; checking that you have understood properly).

    e. offer comforting items (such as food or tea, or a soft pillow) to make your partner feel physically more comfortable.

    f. offer to assume some or all of the burden (e.g., make an offer to field phone calls or to look after children or cook dinner).

    g. offer and give concrete help in terms of time, services, or efforts.

    h. give messages of encouragement or support.

    i. give gifts as comfort or reminders of being loved, marking the specialness of your feelings for the other and of your alliance when the other needs reminding (these can be actual gifts or messages, such as cards or flowers, or can be gifts of service or effort such as special meals).

    j. validate feelings through words (e.g., 'I would feel just the same', or 'Of course that's what you would say/do/need/feel').

    k. give encouragement or praise.

l. validate your partner's sense of worth in words (e.g., 'I love you'/'You're the sane one'/'They don't know what they're missing').

m. perform acts which are enabling to your partner (e.g., chopping wood for fire to warm him/her; fixing the fuse when the lights go out; taking your car in to be serviced to ensure his/her safety, paying joint bills for him/her).

2. On recognising moments of particular feeling and wishing to indicate the specialness of your alliance, you:

a. show this through gifts or celebratory gestures.

b. demonstrate it through physical gestures, such as hugs, kisses, pats, affectionate stroking.

c. listen empathically, indicating shared pleasure through smiles, nods, encouragement to tell the story or expand on the pleasure.

d. offer to enable further success, if relevant (e.g., 'If you need some time to write up an addendum to that report, I'll make dinner').

Protection is the opposite of character attacks, contempt, unrelenting criticism, undermining and a repeated onslaught without regard to the effect on your partner.

The story of Jackie and Obi

Jackie and Obi, both of African origin but born in Britain, have been together for eleven years. They are both 32. Although not married (because they cannot afford the huge party which, according to African tradition, would be expected of them by their vast numbers of relatives), they have been through a traditional African betrothal ceremony. They have one three-year-old daughter, Atalanta, on whom they dote. Jackie is training to be a teacher, having formerly worked in banking, while Obi is an accountant at a large, prestigious accounting firm. They met at university, where Jackie was doing a post-graduate course and Obi finishing a law degree. Although they are a very happy couple now, their early years were marked by Obi's ambivalence. They also have endured a miscarriage and harassment and vandalism by a disturbed neighbour which was so brutal and protracted that it drove them to court, to a point of discord in which Jackie walked out briefly, and eventually to moving house. And, like most of the five couples who are prominently featured in the documentary series on Channel 4, they did not come from families in which their parents had happy, fulfilling, or particularly stable marriages.

Unlike some of the other happy couples, Jackie and Obi do not talk about 'falling in love at first sight'. Instead, the acknowledged commitment to a long-term relationship took years to develop, mostly because of Obi's ambivalence about being committed to anyone. At the beginning Jackie took the initiative; because Obi was already seeing someone else, it took a few months for him to realise that Jackie was more than a friend – both in her eyes and his own. For six months at university and four years afterwards they saw each other but did not live together. Jackie, again, took the initiative here by buying her own flat. They moved in together, but even then Jackie was not sure that Obi was committed to a future with her, and Obi himself admits these doubts.

Their early arguments reflected this ambivalence: Obi would want to spend time with his friends, excluding Jackie, and both attached great importance to being 'right' – that is, to getting his or her own way. Each wanted to avoid the feeling that the other could 'control' him or her. Each perceived the other as 'strong-willed' and 'stubborn'. The guiding principle of their relationship had not yet become what it is now: to avoid hurting the other. The route to their solid sense of partnership, in which the other's interests are taken as seriously as your own, was not smooth. 'In the early days it was pretty rocky,' remembers Obi. 'I think it was just the fact that you don't really have your own space and you've got to get used to sharing things with someone else and . . . their habits. That sort of caused a few ructions in the early days . . . There was a sort of a clash of personalities.' They clashed over the right way to do things, how much time and attention each was prepared to give to the other, over whether Obi was taking Jackie's needs seriously enough and whether Obi was being given enough space.

When Jackie became pregnant for the first time they experienced a shift in priorities. It was this event which made Obi acknowledge what he had been avoiding: that he wanted to spend the rest of his life with Jackie, and he had to make her more central, make her, rather than his friends, the highest priority. The guiding principle changed from doing what you want, getting your own way and being right, to being a partnership, with your partner the person you need to protect, in part to promote your common aims in your joint project (in their case, their creation of a family), and in part because you have come to care for and attend to the other person. The underlying reason the shift could be made was that Obi was motivated to seek security and comfort, and had come to recognise that he would get that best in the context of a stable family life.

'My mother died when I was two,' says Obi. 'My parents had moved to England from Nigeria, but as is sometimes the custom in Nigerian families my older sister remained in Nigeria with another part of the family for a while and then came over. There was a good deal of going back and forth to Nigeria, including my going back there with another sister for secondary school, to a boarding school there. My father married again, then divorced, and is married a third time now. I think, in reaction to all this, I have always craved security, and can see that I want and need a secure family.' In fact, instead of being a barrier to stability, in this case his early history of family instability formed the foundation for his dedication as an adult to family security. It was a question of

when Obi felt ready to declare himself part of a family. Part
of what had been difficult for him at first was that he wanted
to feel adequate to the task: he wanted to be secure financially,
so that he could '. . . give my family the security I wanted for
them.'

Jackie describes Obi as being 'very cautious. Very
responsible, and even conservative. He stops me being flighty
– like I'll make a daft suggestion, not really thinking about
it, and he will bring me down to reality. He takes his time
and considers things very carefully.' Until Jackie's pregnancy,
Obi 'took things one step at a time . . . I said, "Okay, let's
move in together, but we'll take it one step at a time",' he
says about their first move towards commitment. For her part,
Jackie knew from the earliest days that she could make a life
with him. He says that Jackie has always known that having
a stable and secure family life was desirable and possible.
'Her family was much more settled and stable – one mother,
one father.' But Jackie points out that she also had cause to
doubt: her mother's business ventures took her back to Africa
frequently and sometimes for long periods. Partly in reaction,
Jackie also made security, stability and consistency high
priorities.

In the end Jackie miscarried, (although a few years later
Atalanta, now three, was born) but before this they celebrated
their betrothal, thus publicly and privately declaring that they
were a family. They also soon moved into a jointly owned
house, rather than Jackie's solely owned flat. As Jackie
describes it: 'I don't know, it just sort of was "well, we're
starting a family, so it's all different now, isn't it?" ' Buying
this house itself also pushed Obi into further commitment,
but the events leading up to the decision to do so also made
an impact.

For a number of months, a disturbed neighbour had not
only been harrassing them, but she had been threatening
Jackie, and because she had a criminal record and connections
she made good on some of them: things were stolen and

destroyed in their flat, and Jackie in particular felt very unsafe, and especially so when she became pregnant. A court case, which they won, and resulting in an injunction against the neighbour, did little to allay the fear. Jackie wanted to move; Obi's cautiousness got in the way. He argued that it would be a financial disaster and so they should wait. The disagreement escalated and Jackie walked out. In the interim both calmed down and saw the situation in the light of the other's argument. Jackie returned, ready to make peace and offer to wait, even though she felt insecure. But Obi had changed his mind, having decided that his partner and child's feelings of safety (he was not sure that, at that point, they were actually unsafe, but conceded perhaps that was debatable) were the most important things. And, as if they had some guardian angel watching above on that day, interest rates went down. Soon they were buying their first house together.

It was at that point they admitted their relationship projected into a long-term future together. 'Buying the house together made the relationship more equal, more of a partnership,' says Jackie. That sense of partnership, of being allies in their most important venture together, took over. 'Before,' recalls Jackie, thinking about the days before they faced having children together and before buying a jointly owned house, 'we used to do what we wanted, but now we do actually consider each other . . . he does think about what I'm going to think about . . . and I think about what he's going to say before I do something.' Obi would go off on holiday with his mates before; now, at this point in his life, that would not appeal. Obi corroborates this by commenting that 'anything (now) I do for myself is for Jackie, because we're a unit now, so you can't just make a decision without taking Jackie into consideration.'

At the turning point of Jackie's pregnancy, Obi also realised that he could trust her, for they had been through rough times and had stayed together. They had endured, by then, the bitterness of the problem with their neighbour. That 'tells you that your relationship is strong – you know, for good or for bad, you know that you're prepared to stick with someone, your partner, even when you're way down low.' The sense of security that Jackie gave him, and the knowledge, as he took stock, that he could give her the same, helped Obi to shift his priorities, so that now protection is the overriding theme of this couple's relationship.

This gets expressed in the following ways. First, they are both committed to the central enterprise of their lives, creating a stable and secure family, and this enterprise is a joint one. They are allies, dependent on each other in the deepest sense. Jackie, who is very gregarious and has many friends, says Obi often asks her 'Who is your best friend – because sometimes he might think one of my girlfriends might be my best friend. I always say, "no, you're my best friend! And if anything ever goes wrong it's always you I turn to . . . not my parents, even . . . it's always you first." ' And Obi says, 'I know the way Jackie thinks. I know the way her mind works. And sometimes she shows that she knows what I'm thinking – you know, something will happen and she'll say, "I know what Obi's thinking at this point." And she's right.'

Jackie agrees: 'Sometimes when we're out and something catches my eye, I'll say, "Oh, did you notice that?" and he'll say, "Yes, I did. I was just about to say that to you" . . . I can't put my finger on it, but when things happen he thinks exactly the same way. Or if he thinks somebody's really odd or picks up on something from a conversation, I will have picked up on the same thing as well. It's not like we're telepathic or anything, but we do think alike to a certain degree.'

Obi elaborates: 'She's my best friend, you know . . . I can talk to her about anything. We have no secrets.' And Jackie says, 'We always talk to each other. Sometimes for a whole week we might be really, really busy and we haven't really had a good discussion, and I'll say, "Turn off the television. Let's talk about this. Let's have a good chinwag," because we haven't had a good discussion in a long time.' In saying this, Jackie is reporting how she is working to monitor their relationship, to make the effort to combat the force of inertia or drift which can undermine their joint enterprise as a couple. And, unlike before their shift towards a protective relationship, now most of their social life is shared. 'My best friend's Atalanta's godfather, and I'm godfather to his son and Jackie's going to be godmother to their new daughter. And we have other friends, couples who we go out with, but it's usually together.' Sharing this common pursuit gives them a steel bond.

Atalanta, their three-year-old daughter, is the living product of that bond. According to Obi, 'She's like proof positive that, yes, this is the relationship; we've got a relationship there, let's have a child and that's proof that the relationship is working, you know.' She binds them together. 'We have to make decisions about Atalanta, and so most of the decisions we make for the future obviously concern Atalanta and she therefore affects our relationship . . . she's just like the completion of it.'

Out of that intense and profound bond comes a sense of partnership which is central to their individual identities. Jackie describes with amused affection how sometimes it is hard for Obi to be left alone without her: 'I know that he feels lonely if I'm not around. Say, like, during this week, I had to go to my brother's house because my computer had broken down and I had to do some work. And Obi was moaning all evening: it was, "Oh, make sure you give Atalanta her dinner," and I thought, "I always give Atalanta her dinner," and then, "Oh, can't you take Atalanta with you?" And I said, "No. The only time you ever do this is when I'm going out by myself and you're not with me." He goes, "Well, I don't really want to admit it, but I'm going to miss you." I said, "I'm only going for a couple of hours. I'll be back soon." And even when I got there I phoned him to say I'd reached there and I phoned him to tell him I was leaving and on my way home.' Jackie and Obi both describe Obi as a very self-possessed and capable man, obviously able to endure a few hours on his own. What this 'missing' Jackie is about is feeling so deeply connected to another that you feel a part of yourself is gone when that person leaves.

This means a continual sense of the other, sometimes like a hum in the background. Jackie describes this: 'I always think of him. I think, "Is he going to get to the station on time? I'm going to tell him this and that." ' And Obi describes the sense of not being quite at home with himself if he does not feel in tune with Jackie: 'If we've had an argument and I'm worrying about it the next day I find I can't think straight, to be honest. I've just got to make it work. But when I'm sure everything at home is okay I can get on.' To this end, Obi has set a ground rule: conflicts are sorted out before they go to bed or dropped. This seems to work. And they can drop conflicts or easily sort them out because the priority has shifted from the need to be right to the need to get along. Jackie describes some of how this works for her: 'Sometimes I think, "Oh, I could really say something. I could really hurt you." But I'm not going to say it. You don't want to hurt the other person's feelings, so you just don't say it.' To do so is taboo. This is making the effort, or what is sometimes called 'work' in relationships. To be impulsive could mean to be hurtful.

The clarity of their perspective, that the partnership is the first priority, with individual identities significantly defined by the partnership, makes it much easier to be able to think protectively about each other. If your self-identity and self-esteem are centrally tied up with your partnership you think of your partner as almost yourself, as automatically as you do about your child, or at times even *before* yourself. As Obi has said, decisions are almost never independent of Jackie. This sometimes gets expressed as in the following: 'You don't think about only yourself; you're thinking about what would Obi say about this, or how would this affect him.' It also can be expressed as something akin to telepathy. That is, knowing your partner so well, you can tell what he will be thinking or doing, or having the same thoughts and reactions, as both Jackie and Obi reported above.

The shift for Jackie and Obi toward a pivotal partnership has also allowed each to expose to the other his or her vulnerability. Each trusts that the other will be protective and will look after the other. 'We both think about each other a lot,' says Obi. 'I mean, if Jackie's sort of doing something out of the ordinary, you know, you worry. You think, "Oh, I wonder how Jackie's getting on." And other times you just think about what she's doing, because most of the time we know exactly where the other is. Like, when she was working I could go, I know, oh yeah, she's in the office. When she's at school or going out to the university I think, oh, I wonder what she's doing now.'

This monitoring, or wondering about the other, produces a sense of concern about each other's security and safety: 'When I go out I do tend to ring, for instance if I'm going out for a drink after work, just so she doesn't worry.' When Jackie was working in banking and miserable in her job, she would phone Obi a good deal. Obi says, 'We used to have our 11.30 phone call . . . We just used to chat, say what's been going on. Just to touch base. Just to feel you're close. And even if she wasn't in work, if she was at home, I'd ring home. And then we'd call again in the afternoon.' This touching base and feeling close reassured both of them, and if for any reason the phone call was missed they would worry, or feel out of sorts.

What also has evolved is an interdependence so that one complements the other, and in that sense lifts burdens from him or her. For instance, Obi says that: 'Jackie sort of comes up with ideas, and I sort of say yea or nay; in a way this is looking after me so I don't have to think about it. It takes a lot of pressure off me.' And Jackie says that she looks after Obi by 'taking a lot of the household responsibilities on . . . the cleaning, the cooking, washing, looking after Atalanta to a certain degree. If I have to shoot off early in the morning

Obi does it. But we've kind of split that now, so that he gets her ready in the morning and I make sure that she has her evening meal and goes to bed. So that gives him the freedom to do any work he needs to do in the evening.' While this traditional division of labour is fairly typical of couples with young children, and disquieting in particular to women who had entered relationships assuming a fifty-fifty division of domestic tasks, Jackie is unbothered by it. She accepts it as part of what she does to make their joint life run smoothly, and believes that Obi is working equally hard, making a different contribution. In addition, Jackie is deeply concerned about tidiness ('I even once tidied up my friend's house because it was such a mess; she wasn't upset by it, she was grateful') and Obi is not. After early domestic rows over tidiness, Jackie has accepted that it suits her, even gives her satisfaction, to be in charge of the house. Jackie also looks after the family finances, even though Obi is an accountant. This is to give him a break.

They also look after each other by assuring each other's long-term security. Jackie says that Obi might make long-term financial plans, such as when they might look forward to moving, but that they discuss this grand plan together, in terms of what's best for Atalanta's future as well as their own. When Jackie wanted a career change, as we have seen, she needed to reassure Obi that this would not divert them from their grand scheme: she would get a job as soon as she qualified.

On a more prosaic level each looks after the other's safety. This is partly behind their frequent phone calls. It is also behind the rituals both perform nightly to ensure that the house is safe. Obi locks up, but Jackie 'always makes sure that the house is secure and everything, so . . . if I think that we need fire alarms, I'll say, "I'll buy the fire alarms, you make sure that you put them up." ' Jackie gets a sense of security from 'just knowing he's around, he's there, he's looking after me.' And Obi says he gets security from Jackie 'being there and backing me up in a sense. For instance, looking after Atalanta. I know that I never have to worry about Atalanta because Jackie's always there . . . and I mean, there are certain things that I get a bit lazy about and I can't be bothered to do, and Jackie does it.' This nourishment of security, fostered by trust, forms a key part of protective love.

But protective love can also be expressed in knowing that your partner is your 'cheerleader' – knowing that one person in this world really feels your joy as well as your pain, really wants your success and happiness, and your comfort as much as you wish for it. 'You know, he'll try to help me out of a situation and gives me support,' Jackie says. 'Depending on how I feel about something, he'll try to think like me and if he thinks I'm right he'll agree with me and say, "Look, I'm behind you all the way".' The person who knows you and values this well can also champion your welfare by 'saving you from yourself': Jackie says that Obi provides a grounding for her because she can be 'flighty', while Obi says that he is sometimes too conservative and depends on Jackie to come up with ideas, which he will then consider more deeply than she would. They use each other as sounding boards and for advice. 'Sometimes if there's something in the office that he's not very happy with, he will tell me what's happening and I'll give my opinion, and you know that helps him to get through some tricky times,' Jackie observes.

Obi agrees. But he does the same for her: 'Sometimes she's confident that she knows what she's doing . . . and there are other times when she doesn't have that confidence and she needs me to fall back on. And I provide that . . . I mean, I'm sort of there as a back-up for her.' This echo of support and importance from another is central to fostering love. So Jackie and Obi now express this kind of support, this form of protection, for each other in a number of different ways.

But is all of this seamless, easy? Jackie and Obi talk about how it has become much easier: 'Before, you know, we used to do what we wanted. But now we do actually consider each other . . . It got to a point where we were arguing over the silliest things, and you just get fed up of arguing . . . and so we came to saying, let's sit down, let's talk about it and we would put all our grievances on the table. So I went away and I came to think, "Well, he really doesn't like me doing that, so I'm going to try and make an effort not to do it," and he would do the same,' Jackie recounts.

Slowly, this came to be the habit, which replaced the old one of not thinking about the other and doing things just for oneself. These days, though they have conflicts, they stop them much sooner. As Jackie describes it, 'Now, if we have an argument, it's like it starts off as an argument, and then we just start laughing about it. Someone will say, "Oh, for God's sake, don't be so silly," and then you just start laughing about it. Or somebody will say, "Oh, I was only winding you up!" . . . After a while it became give and take. He would listen . . . I would listen. Now it is a lot of compromise, and I also now think before I come up with a suggestion, I really do think, "Will he approve of it?" ' They have come to trust each other, to be sure that they are not going to hurt each other through arguing.

To reinforce this they have set ground rules, of which we have already seen one but there are others, as well. Ground rules, we will see in Chapter 11, are very important tools in managing conflict. Most successful couples operate them, even if they are not, like Jackie and Obi's, explicit: 'We don't have any argument whereby we're not talking for a week. An argument will last for about ten seconds and that's the end of it . . . There's a rule now that we're never go to bed at night in a bad mood.' They have come to the conclusion that 'it's much more important to talk to each other than it is to be angry and not talk to each other.' Valuing the common goals of the partnership, making the partner feel comfortable and secure increases the individual's comfort and security.

It is at these points of discord that what I have talked about as the self-conscious work of relationships steps in. This is when this couple makes a conscious effort to do the counter-instinctive, rather than the impulsive thing, which is to look after what appears at that moment to be your own self-interest and to defend *against* the partner. As Jackie says, she thinks first about what Obi would think before she proposes something; they call a halt to things before they get out of hand, because they both agree they value the peace between them more than being right, and they stop themselves from saying hurtful things. They also sometimes take a break, to cool off, as Joe and Iona do (see Chapter 7), and then come back more ready to listen.

To assess how protective you are to each other in your relationship, and how you might think about improving it, you can try the following **exercise**:

Take the list of protective behaviours, as reproduced below, and tick how many, first, you think you do, most of the time, for your partner, and then, how you think he or she would answer for you:

1. When you recognise your partner's vulnerability (for instance, his or her insecurity, pain, anxiety, fear, doubt, or disappointment; this can occur either when you are told about it or you when recognise or intuit it from other more inchoate signs), and in recognising it, you:
    a. physically comfort him/her (e.g., put your arms around your partner, hug, stroke, or hold his/her hand).
    b. say comforting or supportive things to him/her.
    c. offer constructive and supportive advice.
    d. listen empathically (as shown by nodding, making eye contact, giving assuring sounds of acknowledgement; giving prompts to go on; checking that you have understood properly).

e. offer comforting items (such as food or tea, or a soft pillow) to make your partner feel physically more comfortable.

f. offer to assume some or all of the burden (e.g., make an offer to field phone calls or to look after children or cook dinner).

g. offer and give concrete help in terms of time, services, or efforts.

h. give messages of encouragement or support.

i. give gifts as comfort or reminders of being loved, marking the specialness of your feelings for the other and of your alliance when the other needs reminding (these can be actual gifts or messages, such as cards or flowers, or can be gifts of service or effort such as special meals).

j. validate feelings through words (e.g., 'I would feel just the same' or 'Of course that's what you would say/do/need/feel').

k. give encouragement or praise.

l. validate your partner's sense of worth in words (e.g., 'I love you'/'You're the sane one'/'They don't know what they're missing').

m. perform acts which are enabling to your partner (e.g., chopping wood for fire to warm him/her, fixing the fuse when the lights go out; taking your car in to be serviced to ensure his/her safety, paying joint bills for him/her).

2. On recognising moments of particular feeling and wishing to indicate the specialness of your alliance you:
   a. show this through gifts or celebratory gestures.
   b. demonstrate it through physical gestures, such as hugs, kisses, pats, affectionate stroking.
   c. listen empathically, indicating shared pleasure through smiles, nods, encouragement to tell the story or expand on the pleasure.

d. offer to enable further success, if relevant (e.g., 'If you need some time to write up an addendum to that report, I'll make dinner').

CHAPTER FOUR

Creating More Protective Love

Gwen and Howard's is a story of the lost opportunity to ask for and to recognise in your partner a need for protection. Theirs is a story about a couple dearly in need of it, besieged by the most painful event of all, the death of a child.

Gwen and Howard lost their son after eight years of chronic illness. The illness, though genetic, did not surface for a year. From that point he was recurrently extremely ill, with frequent hospitalisations. Gwen bore the brunt of his care. She gave up her rewarding work as a teacher, as it became apparent that her very ill child needed her at home. As head of a peripatetic sales force, Howard travelled frequently. He missed many of the health crises and overnight hospital stays, and was on the periphery of their frequent medical consultations. Gwen turned to neighbours for practical help and her mother for emotional support, but, like Jim's wife (see Chapter 3), missed the experience of sharing the emotional burden with her husband.

Gwen found Howard curiously unresponsive, seemingly unaffected by their child's desperate state. Like Jim, the emotional truth was different from the one shown to the world. Like Jim, Howard was expert in displacing the effects of distress. It suited his management of grief to travel, which helped distance the events and the pain. Away at work he could fool himself that the drama of his son's slow death was not unfolding. Only when he returned did the pain surface. But that would be quickly sidelined by Gwen's fury at him, her repeated attacks on his 'selfish and uncaring behaviour'. Any emotions would be deflected into their enormous rows.

As their child's health deteriorated, the couple's emotional distress intensified. The more Gwen screamed abuse at him for not shouldering the burden of day-to-day care, the more furious she made Howard, marginalising him further. Howard now stayed away for most of the time, for he concluded that he was unwanted at home. He convinced himself that it was better for his son to die peaceably with his mother than in a battleground with both his parents. He found a flat for himself, and ultimately began an affair with a colleague. With her, he could despair over his son's life and death, and with her he could describe the depth of his pain. Gwen, who was the one who should have been the one to share and understand his anguish, had become his enemy.

Neither Gwen nor Howard asked the other effectively for help or recognised what the other needed. Resentment and anger only increased their unbearable pain. Neither made the important leap of faith: to believe that the other must be wanting the same as yourself, in what must be a shared set of feelings. With such a perspective, the protective one, a partnership could have developed, and a whole different story could have flowed. But to do this takes great effort, for every time Gwen did or said something which did not meet Howard's need at the moment, and vice versa, each would have had to step back and reinterpret it as not a deliberately hurtful action, but instead one borne of ignorance of how to respond, or of what the partner was needing. This is the protective stance. It assumes a vulnerability and is predicated upon and fosters a partnership. Divorced one year after their son's death, and out of contact with each other for the ensuing ten years, each now has a legacy of two deaths: their child's and that of their marriage.

Yet, there can be another story told here. We heard earlier from John and Nina, who also lost a child, and whose next baby was near death a number of times in her first year, only to emerge with a severe handicap. This couple used each other as a support during these testing times, and still see each other as 'the only ones who really understand' what the pain of the loss and the experience of living with their child's handicap can mean. As we have seen, this couple talked and, in John's words, 'we learned a lot . . . it was the making of us. I learned Nina . . . was very emotional, and I think that has freed me to express my emotions. I learned that she can be strong and independent, which I admire.' We have already heard him say that that was the time they learned to trust each other; he gave up having any secrets from her.

Nina concurs: 'You don't go through what we have and just get on superficially. It deepens you. I think John suffered almost more than I did about the baby. I just wanted to make it up to him. I was very careful around him, he was hurting all over. I learned how strong he can be; how he reacts to something when it's really bad; how, when the chips are down, he can take control and wants to give everything, really. . . . John's a very logical person and I can be emotional, and he talked me through when it got really, really bad. He'd just say, "Hang on, let's think about this: what's the worst that can happen? Let's cope with this one stage at a time." It changed me a lot. I have a different attitude. He's taught me a lot about being calm.'

They were careful with each other, delicate in managing their pain, now exposed to each other. John and Nina, unlike Gwen and Howard, forged a deeper union through their mutual protection in the face of profoundest pain.

The link between the need for relationships and the need for protection

Where does the link between the need for relationship and the need for protection derive from? Perhaps we need to go back to the proverbial basics for the answer. Where did love come from? And so, what does its loss imply?

Our first love is with our parents – first mother, then father. When they step out of the centre of our lives, or we move out of the centre of theirs, there is a space, a vacuum around connection and relationship. All later love is a partial reconstruction of that love and a filling of that vacuum or space, a reconnecting; it has the same impulse as before: to be sure of the connection, to hold it and to be emotionally held by it. The difference is that, as adults, we enter these relationships of love transformed by the fact that we have inner lives which contain our histories, skills and experiences, which mediate the need and desire for that continued total preoccupation and absorption which characterises the earliest mother-child love.

As we have seen, and as attachment theory describes with a strong body of research to bolster the claim, marital love is patterned on, but not the same as, first the love between mother and child, and second, that between father and child. It is thus suffused with expectations that *it is the relationship of final refuge, of ultimate protection.* Nina and John protected each other; they testify to the endurance of their love. Gwen and Howard abandoned each other and their love died.

The corollary requirement of this is that the focus, or beam, shines on the partner, and that this focus is necessary to provide that refuge and protection. Howard's focus went off Gwen, and in turn hers off him, while John and Nina maintained their attention on each other. This attention in their case gradually led to a reordering of priorities on John's part, a transforming of his life, when he sold his business and refocused on his wife and child. He was then in a better position to provide the sort of security and build the trust his family required of him.

Most commonly, the expectation in married love that your spouse will look after your vulnerability remains unspoken and, worse, unacknowledged. This was the mistake of Gwen and Howard. Neither asked for help, neither admitted vulnerability to the other. Distance, for Howard, and anger, for Gwen, replaced it. Each replaced attributions of protective interest one might have for the other with attributions of self-interest and retaliation. Related to this is the unspoken expectation that your spouse cares enough about you to look out for your interests and feelings, in many ways just as your parents did (or you yearned for them to do). Nina, according to John, knows him so well she 'reads' his moods and energy levels before she makes a suggestion, but John also is giving her information. By talking, communicating with her, keeping the lines open, John assumes responsibility for Nina's knowledge of him. Because of this, she can at times do without explicit information and 'read' him correctly with excellent consistency. Much of the disappointment in relationships stems from a spouse's failure to 'read' correctly, or his or her alleged failure to do it. And yet people are unconscious of this until they begin to feel resentful.

Then, to complicate things even further there is the gender divide: how to get around the problem that men and women show love in such different ways? How do men and women manage to cross the divide and love each other?

In short, men and women, respectively, when happily married, are filling the vacancy left by the parent from childhood – whether the actual good parent or the wished-for good one. Nina leans on John; she knew he could be relied upon to deal with the doctors while she was in surgery, she knows he helps her to organise her thinking ('. . . let's take this one step at a time') when she is upset ('I've learned how to be calm from him'). John also leans on Nina; he knows she will support him with her sensitivity to his moods and that her affectionate ways and fiery spirit release him to be more affectionate and emotional. Part of the reason for their marital happiness is that they continue to give that sense of protection, focus and gratitude which we all need even when we leave childhood, as either the mother or father would or should have given.

In other words, we all carry around expectations of Idealised-Males-as-Protectors and Idealised-Females-as-Protectors, based in part on our experiences of mothers and fathers and in part on our cultural definitions of what these should be. In the happy couples, we see that the men and women respectively step into those roles more successfully than unhappy couples.

Obi and Jackie's relationship emanates protectiveness towards each other. When Jackie describes what Obi does for her, this sense of being protected, of leaning on his 'big shoulders' is emphasised: 'I don't really reel safe when he's not around. If he's not home till late I find it hard to settle down. It's not that I'm not independent, and I can be on my own' (they, in fact, sometimes take separate vacations). 'It's just that much more secure when I feel he's home and can protect me.' As we know, Jackie and Obi once lived near a neighbour who frightened Jackie, and during that period Obi's presence was particularly important. For his part, even though at that point it would have meant a financial hardship for them to move, Obi decided that for Jackie's sense of security they should do so.

But Obi also says that Jackie is essential to his sense of security. She listens to him, for he saves up his observations and experiences of his day at work to tell her (as she does for him); he knows she is thinking about him and worrying about his safety and that he can rely on her to be concerned for him; he relies on her to ease his burdens, as he knows she will be thinking, 'What does he need and how can I help?' – that she will be trying to read him and doing things for him; that she will be concerned that he is eating properly and try to look after this for him; that she will be monitoring what can be done around the house to make it a comfortable home.

Most social scientists do agree that there is a masculine experience and a feminine one, without necessarily ascribing a final cause to this condition – nature or nurture. Masculine and feminine qualities underlie our heterosexual attractions to each other, and perhaps they also underlie what makes great relationships work, despite my earlier implication that the gender difference is what divides us. In our earliest relationships – with our parents – we seek nurturance, safety and protection, feeding and attention or focus. At first the mother, the caretaker of the infant, assures these, often with help from her partner, who is most often the father. When there is a father, the caretaking, as the nature of it changes, also assumes some of these functions.

But children receive care differently from men and women, and learn to expect and seek different forms of it from their fathers and mothers. Children feel looked after by fathers whom they believe in large part to be men who provide a sense of safety, competence and confidence in managing the real, harsh world outside. Loved and idealised fathers – and commonly small children compete with each other over who has the 'best father' in just these words – are 'bigger/stronger/smarter/more powerful than your father/anyone else in the world'. These men have jobs which the children usually idealise as very important, which help to keep the household going (and very often the children believe that the father's job is the more lucrative or important than the mother's, even if it is not). Fathers are also usually relied on to fix things, carry heavy objects and provide protection against the elements because they are normally bigger and stronger. Children feel they are loved by their fathers, but in this way.

In contrast, mothers are idealised for being 'kind', 'nice', 'listening', and 'understanding'. Mothers love children by looking after their daily feeding, clothing and social needs and by making time to listen and talk to them. In truth, both men and women who are loving can provide a bit of all these different categories of protective love, for either sex has capacities to do so. It is the balance which differentiates them.

And so, in adult love we can also provide both kinds: Nina, for instance, being strong for John when he is in the throes of ME and depression, being calm and logical, which, she says she learned from him, and John being soft and affectionate for Nina, which he says he learned from her. But the balance still tips in different directions according to gender in the kind of protective love we do provide. When we grow up and away we leave our idealised parents. If we have had anything like them as children we yearn for them again. If we have not had anything nearly like them as children we go on yearning to have them now. So, as adults, we meet someone and fall in love, and we love men who can love us with the shadows of our ideal fathers cast over that love, and women who love us with the shadows of our ideal mothers.

Yet for many, gender divides rather than bridges the gap. So what do you do about it? What you do underscores the point (made in the Introduction) that achieving a properly protective and happy relationship takes a good deal of conscious and unspontaneous effort. This is the main 'work' which people speak of when they talk about 'working at relationships'. It is what we saw Jackie and Obi learn to do. It means doing the counter-instinctive thing; the instinctive response when facing difficulties, complexities and divisions between people is to protect self-interest. The counter-instinctive approach is to suppress these impulses, so that a more comprehensive perspective which emphasises the part-nership and each person's potential to be hurt can be held in mind.

First, you need to be self-conscious again: to change the perspective from self-preservation to shared goals and responses, that your partner is like you. He feels the same. You may have disappointed him. He probably has disappointed you. Fallible, you are also improvable. Second, you need consciously to change your behaviour in three key potentially divisive areas of interaction with your partner: a. making efforts to improve your means of communication; b. making efforts at managing conflict; and c. making an effort to manage and sustain that most intimate part of your relationship, sex, with delicacy and wisdom, as these next sections will try to explain.

Protection and communication

One of the more frequent findings in marital research is that couples value the ability to communicate well with their partners. The ability to communicate clearly is key to establishing intimacy, for it allows people to understand what is 'inside' them. Social historians have pointed out that conversation between people is a key enterprise of humanity, because it is central to the quest to ease loneliness.[1]

According to most research on what people say they value in their partners, the pivotal concept in our current marital ideal is that your partner is 'your best friend'. This seems to mean someone with whom you can exchange intimate thoughts and feelings, and to whom you can talk freely. Both men and women cite this as a necessary quality when they are asked in studies to evaluate their marital satisfaction. What they seem to mean is the ability to feel safe in saying what they want to say, as much as feeling that they will be understood.

Since men less frequently make use of this quality (and sometimes never do) it must be the quality of feeling that one *can* speak freely without repercussion and with understanding, rather than the actual practice of doing so which is so important. If you fear dire consequences from self-disclosure or judgemental criticism from revelation you will cease to talk directly and openly and communication begins

71

to break down or becomes distorted. It is the safety, the feeling that the listener will protect you in your disclosures which may be central to the ability to disclose. As researchers on communication in families have documented[2] distorted communication patterns (that is, unclear and indirect ones) are highly associated with dysfunction in families. So, in this sense, feeling safe, or protected, is connected to communicating well and vice versa. The couples who are happy report that it is the comfort of being able to say or do anything – to be yourself – which is so valuable.

'We talk all the time. We talk about anything. I'll ring Jackie during the day just to tell her about something that just happened at the office. When we get home we tell each other what else has happened,' says Obi. Watching them throughout the week this is corroborated. This couple follows each other around talking, telling stories, making light jokes with each other, registering small complaints and irritations and laughing with each other. It is a verbal and easy atmosphere.

Successful couples have learned how to:

1. *ask for*
2. *graciously receive*
3. *interpret their partner's need for protection more correctly* (although, being human, they are not infallible in interpreting others' wishes or meeting others' needs, as Winnicott described when he identified and exalted 'good enough mothering'[3])

So, for instance, John says that Nina helped him recover through a very long bout of ME and depression. 'It would be that most days I could barely function, but there would be a few okay days sprinkled in between. During those good days I managed to be able to talk to Nina and tell her what I needed, which was to be left alone when I was really out of it but chivvied along when there was a little energy. So when I would collapse again and have a bad day she wouldn't badger me the way some people might have, and when I showed a little bit of life she would make gentle suggestions about doing things, which I might or might not take up. If I said no she never pushed it, she followed my lead.'

Nina did not get it right all the time. 'Sometimes she would suggest something and I would be so irritable I would snap at her. On the good days I had the resources to apologise. But she gradually learned just how much to offer and just how much to step back – she learned how to "read" my moods and needs more correctly.' But John had taken the responsibility first. Now, her 'reading' is well-informed, because of his disclosure and openness.

As an exercise in self-assessment you can ask yourself how you and your partner rate on this kind of communication. Try to remember a recent time when you had to ask your partner for something difficult (it could be a favour, or a change in his or her attitude, or behaviour). Can you remember how you asked? Was your request direct and clear, or masked and perhaps circuitous? Did it take into account how your partner might have heard it? Could he or she have been threatened, challenged or made insecure by it – in other words, were you not being at all protective of your partner's vulnerability? If you asked clearly, directly and protectively, it is much more likely that your request was taken on board.

Can you, on the other hand, remember receiving your partner's help recently? How did you receive it? 'Graciously receiving' shows an acknowledgement and appreciation of the help. It actually takes courage to do this and it is something which often slips away in habitual relationships, to their detriment.

And, finally, can you think of a time when you thought your partner needed help, support or assistance, and, in retrospect, you realise that you failed to notice it? Such failure is a failure to put yourself fully in his or her shoes; a failure of trying to imagine what it must feel like for the other, who, after all is probably more like you than you admit. The point of this exercise is that we all fail our partners now and again; preoccupation, illness, exhaustion, poorly managed conflict and poor communication all make that likely. But choosing to try to repair when it goes wrong, which the next section addresses, and to take a protective perspective in general, can make all the difference. Another way in which couples can become more protectively loving is in the way they manage the inevitable conflicts between them.

Protection and the management of conflict

Conflict means there is a break in feeling protected and properly focused upon. It diminishes the potential for grateful feelings and balance. The happy couples manage to come back to an upward spiral, even despite temporary breaks in it (for conflict, by definition, means a break, being on an opposite side). The unhappy couples experience, by contrast, a continuing break in empathy; they occupy opposite sides of a permanent wall, supported by gender differences.

Conflict, as a set of recent studies have shown, is not harmful in itself, as it opens up and stretches relationships. Through it, people become more intimate, learning more about themselves through the points of difference which are like large or small shocks which arouse them to new and important information about the other, or make them take the other in instead of routinely rubbing alongside without true notice of each other. It is not conflict, therefore, *per se*, which erodes love but how it is managed[4].

These studies highlight the salience of being *able to air differences or acknowledge conflicts* within a couple, and of resolving them in a variety of healthy and constructive ways. There are a few ways to be constructive:

1. Some couples agree to disagree after airing their differences
2. Others have major set-to's, heated at first, then gradually

calming down enough to reason their way, respectfully, together through their differences, often coming up with a compromise, sometimes one person's view prevailing

3. Others by-pass the heated emotional scene, and go straight to reasoned discussion.

In all three cases, it is *the ability to air differences in a style which suits them* which enables a couple to maintain a loving stance towards each other. The ability to do this is central to the endurance of happiness between couples.

Where do your and your partner fit in this typology? Is one person one kind and the other another? This makes the task harder, but not impossible: it means sometimes you will settle things one way, sometimes another, most likely. John and Irene, whom we meet in Chapter 6, maintain that they never exchange a cross word. Margaret and Mark have infrequent explosions, as do Nina and John and Jackie and Obi, while Joe and Iona's (see Chapter 7) outbursts are a bit more frequent. In all cases these outbursts and conflicts are accepted, processed and not allowed to fester. Some reach a compromise, as Jackie and Obi maintain they do ('we talk it out until we reach some kind of a solution, (sometimes) a compromise,' reports Jackie). Others decide that, after listening to both sides, the other partner can be right, because nothing really matters that much (this is the style favoured by Joe and Iona and Mark and Margaret). John and Irene do not even let things get to a point of expressed conflict: usually John will come to the point of thinking Irene is right, in any case; it doesn't matter if he doesn't get his way, and as they share most of the same values, he can trust her to be right.

The studies also suggest that beneath these healthy pathways to managing differences are a variety of additional factors, such as *avoiding* the following:

1. recriminations
2. character assassination
3. persistent criticism

4. taking a consistently defensive stance

Avoiding all four of these relate to the idea of protective love. They are each about avoiding hurting someone who is most vulnerable to you; anyone who has surrendered to you in love is by definition particularly vulnerable to you. They also depend on a person's ability to be calm enough to make choices. One choice is to see things differently; that is, to reframe what has looked like a hostile motive into something more benign. So instead, for instance, of thinking, 'My partner is so pigheaded he's just trying to defeat me', you reframe it to, 'I wonder what he is worried about, worried enough to try to defend himself against something he imagines I'm going to do to him?' This strategy, called 'reframing' and discussed further in Chapter 11, is one of the key techniques for turning your relationship around. If you can keep reframing your partner's motives into ones which are consonant with his or her ultimate goal to be in a protective partnership (and vice versa), you are very likely going to face fewer destabilising conflicts.

Nina talks about how she avoided escalating John's irritability when he had ME: 'There were times when he was just so aggressive . . . the best thing I could do was go away, just leave him, visit friends or something. And when I'd come back he'd say, "Oh, I was really a sod this afternoon, wasn't I? I'm so sorry." And I would say, "I know, I know you didn't want to be like it." ' Nina did not expect a conflict-free relationship. Instead, she tried to read what it was John was feeling and did not become defensive, but gently removed herself, and thereby also the possibility of escalation. This took the heat out of the moment and allowed for the later healing to occur with some ease. Chapters 11 and 12 in Part Two go into these strategies in some detail, for they form some of the ground rules for not inflicting harm and so preserving protective love. Another couple once related their own rather ingenious strategy for making up: they maintain a chart on which is recorded who made the first move in their last contretemps. When they have their next conflict, they consult the chart and it is up to the other to take his or her turn to initiate the repair. This may sound contrived, but the most difficult part for many is making a peace overture. By ritualising it the awkwardness disappears; in addition, this strategy ritualises the point that it's less important to be right than to return to feeling united.

In short, happy couples manage conflict, repairing the break and fostering anew the centrality of protection towards each other, while the others fail to do so. The repair facilitates a spiralling upward, a cementing of the relationship, the failure to do so a downward spiral, into resentment, anger and estrangement.

Joe and Iona have been married for 31 years. They are a couple whose faces light up in the presence of each other. To watch them go about their daily routine is to see two people taking great and small pleasures in their partnership: one does the ironing and the other absent-mindedly picks up the folded clothing and puts it away, all the while both keeping up a running set of stories and insights which clearly interest and delight each other. Iona serves an ordinary dinner and Joe kisses her and tells her how much he enjoyed it, while Iona brings him a cup of tea as soon as he comes in from walking the dog. Yet this couple reports that they have frequent, stormy rows.

'Joe has a terrible temper,' says Iona. 'He's better now than he used to be, but he is very quick to get very angry. And I'm not a "yes-person", so these can turn into humdingers!' Joe agrees. 'I'm the volatile one. I just blow my top at times. I'm the fiery one, but then again, Iona can stand her ground and I like that.'

A few years ago Iona felt that the rows had become intolerable. At that time they centred around their older son, who at 28 had not yet left home. Joe says, 'At that time we were just arguing too much over David, our elder son, about stupid things, I suppose: him not being tidy, 28 years of age and still storming around the house. You know it was like living with another man in a small little environment. It was not working. Not for me. I mean, Iona, being a mother and David being her son, I think she had a different feeling towards it all. But me, I couldn't understand that he was still there.'

Joe felt David should have found a place of his own, a steady job and be out of the house. Iona felt much more protectively about this son; she characterises the rows as 'jealousy between the father and son'. Finally, one day she felt she had had enough of Joe's temper and told him he would have to leave.

'I thought about it and thought I could try to live on my own because this kind of arguing was taking too much out of me. Joe went out and found himself a flat, although he told me that if we really were going to split up he would move far away, he wouldn't be staying around. That just about killed me. When I thought about it I knew I couldn't live without him. I realised how alone and sad he felt. It hurt me so much to think of him like that, and I also knew that he was hurting for me. He hadn't actually moved out, so I turned to him and said, "Of course you're not going. Let's not be so silly." All the anger was gone. Then we could talk.' They did talk and eventually their son did leave. Joe reports that his main feeling during the time he thought they might not make it was how much Iona was hurting.

When they have their more mundane arguments there is a pattern they both describe. Joe loses his temper and Iona stands up to him. As Joe describes it, when he feels he is about to go too far he leaves the room. 'I just walk out of the room, or Iona walks out of the room and I go and do something else, and maybe go into my workshop, maybe take the dog for a walk, whatever, you know. I do something maybe for about a quarter of an hour, half an hour, twenty minutes, maybe an hour, and then we go in and I either say I'm very sorry for my behaviour, or, let's talk about this, let's try and get this straightened out . . . We then talk about it and we get it straight. We find something to agree on. We have always thought there must be a way of ironing out the problems. And it's not so important to be right. I think about things when I'm out of the way because I want it to be good – that's my aim. I mean it's no good living a life with someone, spending your days together and nights together and life together, if you're not going to sort out the problems, because you want to be happy together . . . On the walks on my own, or when I'm on my own thinking, I think about Iona, and I love her more (eventually). I felt that I should make it up in some way. I really feel hurt by what I've done to her. It gnaws at my stomach. She always takes me back. She accepts my weaknesses.'

So, after a bit, when Joe takes himself out of the heat, he eventually feels himself calming down. At that point he thinks about Iona, hurting, and thinks, 'What could be worth that?' He then returns, and apologises. When things are calm, apologies made and warm feelings re-established, they discuss things until they both understand the other's feelings and position. They may agree to disagree, or they may compromise. Both *feel* understood, and neither 'feel that it's very important to be right'. Iona says that after Joe leaves, she thinks: 'I know he's going out now to cool off, and he's going to think about me and come back to apologise. I think about him out there alone and feel for him. I might be right, and often I might get my way in the end, but that's not what matters. We both think, during that break time, "Oh, what does it matter? Who cares about being right?" By the time he comes back in we are both feeling better.'

Perhaps most important, however, is that this protectiveness puts the need to be right in the shadows. 'If I think Joe's really upset about something, and I can see he's upset, I really try to think how I can put things right and see his point of view, and talk to him about it, or come to a compromise,' says Iona.

This lack of defensiveness, which results from devaluing the need to be right and prove the other wrong, also enhances the ability to keep other things in perspective. It is a struggle to transform the feeling during conflict that this person crossing you – your partner – is your enemy into the feeling that that same person can be and has been your ally. Iona describes how she does this, but it is very much linked with giving up the need to be deemed right above all else: '. . . I can get to the point at which I think, right, I'm going to leave, I can't take this any more; he's crossed the line again. But then, when I actually think what life might be like (although on the one hand I think, well, it could be a bit of an adventure for me, starting out again), I don't see how I can live without him, because he's so good for me; he's always given me so much confidence. I really can't bear the thought of life without him there.'

Beginning to find a way back to pleasure in each other, they use humour. 'We often end up laughing about it,' they both say, 'although at the time, of course, it's not funny.' But being able to joke about it and knowing that they will is part of the process of recovery and takes the sting out of the arguments. Sometimes the process takes a long time, sometimes it is very quick. Protectiveness, gratitude and memory of pleasure are accessed only after pain and anger subside. The knowledge a break *can* be mended is behind the impulse to repair it.

Sex and the protective function of love

Sex can function either as a seal between a couple or as a divisive force between them. Sex as a bond both stems from and can reinforce the essential elements. Men and women come to sex through opposite routes, and marriage can put them on a fused path[5].

As past research has shown, the psychological task for men in relationships is to bring love into sex[6]. Men first learn to be sexual through an emphasis on their own individual pleasure. They learn about sex as desire before they learn about sex as an expression of love. Normally, their earliest sexual experience is masturbatory. Arousing images of women which are part of masturbatory fantasies objectify women; relationships are not part of early sexual experience for men. Instead, for men, love has to be built into sex, through learning through experience.

For women, the process is the opposite, as this same research indicates. They have to learn to distinguish desire from fantasies about love. For women, erotic feelings are first labelled as romantic ones, and embedded in relationship fantasies. Masturbation typically comes later for women than men, and even more typically, after they have been in long relationships. Women typically have to learn about sex as separate from love.

It is through relationships that these routes begin to merge. Respectively, men and women learn about the merging of sex and love, on the one hand, and the separation of the two, on the other, through the experience of relationship. So, in marriage these opposite routes come together. More to the point, the vulnerability men and women each have – to be 'guilty' of objectifying sex on the one hand, and to be 'guilty' of not claiming desire, on the other – are part of the exposure men and women risk in a relationship such as marriage.

But this is only one form of such exposure. Sex is 'naked' in many ways beyond the physical. Fantasies, especially when revealed to your partner, expose people to every sort of imagined ridicule. Your feelings about your body become a shared business; your partner becomes responsive to how you feel about your body. Sex is above all an arena in which people can feel very vulnerable. As marriage should provide protection, if in the sexual arena it does not, pain, resentment, and anger can result, instead of gratitude and balance. In addition, for sex to grow in pleasure, it needs the quality of focus as well. And so sex can often be the crucible for the upward or downward spiralling of a marriage.

Nina and John have been together for sixteen years, and they still cannot keep their hands off each other. 'I still fancy him rotten,' Nina gushes, eyes lighting up wickedly. John adds, 'Sex is still great. I make a game of pretending she's too much for me; she's younger than I am, and I play at being the old man who can't keep up with her insatiable appetite, but that's become part of the sexual game, the sort of flirting part of it, we play. There's never been a time when we haven't fancied each other and our sex life is fantastic.'

Part of the secret? 'Nina never feels insulted if I am too tired, and I wouldn't be either. We know we fancy each other. She's sensitive to me and my moods,' says John. Nina says, 'No, I never feel "rejected". I know we'll have sex, or a cuddle, or whatever, soon, at some point. I know I fancy John and he fancies me.' This couple feels safe, secure with each other. They do so because they take a longer-term perspective than many couples do: if Nina's advances are rebuffed she '. . . know(s) that (she) will have sex or a cuddle or whatever, soon, *at some point*' (my italics). This perspective emphasises the partnership, the joint enterprise as allies projecting into a shared future. It also forgives the partner, and in this sense is protective.

Irene and John (see Chapter 6), have been married for 23 years. With a sly grin, Irene answers a question about how they would manage any separation (these are infrequent, in any case): 'We'd go straight upstairs,' she says, gesturing with her head towards the bedroom. Irene and John are frequently demonstrative with each other. Watching them banter and discuss things, you are struck by how much of the time they touch, or put arms around each other, or give each other a hug or kiss. They also compliment each other on the way they look, as well as show support ('Irene got me out of my gloom when I was unemployed by telling me how much she believed in me, and how much I had,' says John).

Both these couples are, in consequence, very secure that each partner esteems the other, feels safe with the other and continually is attractive to the other. This security is what can inform confidence. Nina, for instance, has claimed that she is robust against John's rebuffs. For these couples there has been a build-up of protective behaviour, in which each has been reassuring the other about their value and attractiveness.

Another thing these couples mention is that they talk about sex; they are not embarrassed by it or by their desires. They talk about what attracts them to other people, without trying to make the other feel insecure. Nina comments: 'I know what kind of woman John fancies. I know what will make him interested. Sometimes, at a party, I will be talking to some woman and say to her, "Oh, come on over here and meet my husband – he'd really like you!" I don't mean it as some kind of come-on type of thing, but that I know he'd get pleasure out of it and I like seeing that. John does the same with me.'

Knowing that the other is sexually alive fuels their attraction to each other. As a vicar once said to me, 'Seeing an attractive woman walk down the street affects me with pleasure the way it would any man – being spiritual does not mean you're dead.' And similarly for Nina and John, being faithful and in love with each other does not mean they are dead; rather that their sexuality is alive. The result of all this is a satisfying, secure and playful sexual relationship, a source of fun and pleasure continually renewed.

One potential hazard sex brings about is its mundanity over many years in a relationship, which results for many in a decline in both frequency and satisfaction particularly in the middle and later years of marriage. This state of dissatisfaction can jeopardise the protective functions of love, through a build-up of resentment within the couple. One way around this is to use fantasy, to keep flirting, as John and Irene do, and another is to view the change in the sexual relationship as the whole relationship matures as not a loss (of excitement and novelty) but a gain – of a deepened sensitivity to the other's moods and pleasures.

Nina's comments demonstrate just this: 'I think actually sexually we know each other very well now . . . We can separate sex and love, too, and put them back together again . . . I think perhaps reading somebody the way we have done over the years, it becomes like an instinct. When we want to be loving and when we just want to be sexy – we know. You don't actually want to have to say certain things. John just seems to know just what I want at that moment in time and I just find that quite amazing, really, that he can read me that well.'

And the same is true for Irene and John. Irene says that after 23 years of marriage sex is even better than at the start, when they were young, although it was always wonderful: 'I think of it really as making love. I feel that John is really showing me how much he loves me, by doing things which he knows I like and by being patient and gentle. He has learned these things. And I show him in exactly the same way. And you know, everyone has parts of their bodies which they can't stand, which they think are horrible. John loves every part of my body.' That takes time for people to know, to trust in and understand each other. 'That's why I think of it as making love, as really showing his love for me, not as just sex. Though I still tingle when I think of him, or I can still gaze at him and feel butterflies in my stomach' (like when she was younger and saw sex more as lust).

For many couples, sex often becomes mundane and un-satisfying, through the course of long marriages. As research shows, this can not only pose a risk to general marital happi-ness, especially for men, but also for having an affair, for both men and women[7]. (While the relationship between having affairs and feelings about one's spouse is not a simple one, there is evidence that affairs grow out of a disillusionment in marriage and also can contribute to potential instability within it.) Again, there is a gender divide in discussions of sex. Given that men more naturally think of sex as a function apart from a relationship while women see it as part of a relationship and only secondarily as a function, they will feel different things about changes in their sex lives, and use a different kind of language (men: 'I'm not getting any'; women: 'I'm feeling rejected'/'I'm not feeling very loving'.)

Sex can also be a powerful way to re-establish the sense of alliance and protection at the base of a happy relationship. As Judith, a 45-year-old teacher, tells her story of recovery after mastectomy this becomes clear: 'When I had my mastectomy I felt my body was ugly, even though I had had reconstructive surgery. Your breasts are never really right even though you look okay in clothing. I was sure that my husband thought they were disgusting. I didn't feel much like sex for a few months after the surgery, as you can imagine, and he didn't push me. After a while, I began to think it wasn't just me, but maybe it was him: maybe he was so turned off by my body that he couldn't bring himself to make love with me. I asked him and he said, "Well, to be honest, I don't think your breasts are beautiful, but you don't either (which was actually okay to hear because it was true, and so now out in the open between us) but that doesn't make any difference. It wasn't your breasts that made me want you; it's you. If you want me to come to love them because you do I will try. But I haven't stopped loving you, as opposed to a set of breasts, or desiring you!" I realised it was my own rejection of my body, which I assumed he must also be having which was standing in the way; his desire for me has healed me unimaginably. I never think about these not very beautiful, but nevertheless shape-giving, things any more. I feel my body is essentially lovable again.' Judith had been married, essentially, happily for twenty years, when this occurred. Now, two years later, she feels 'happier with my husband than ever, through his affirmation of me, in part.'

It is important to remember that sex can be the scene of

the most hurtful things between men and women, but also the most healing and loving. It is a powerful tool for rebuilding, as the couples' stories here have shown.

To get an idea of whether sex is something which may be potentially (or already) dividing you or uniting you, how would you answer the following questions about your sexual satisfaction and the resilience of your sex life? How would your partner? How similar are your assessments? (Key: 1 = very dissatisfied; 2 = somewhat dissatisfied; 3 = sometimes dissatisfied/sometimes satisfied; 4 = somewhat satisfied; 5 = very satisfied):

1. I am happy with the frequency of my sex life with my partner 1 2 3 4 5
2. I am happy with the amount of fun in my sex life with my partner 1 2 3 4 5
3. I think my partner and I have developed a language of sex – we know how to show each other what we each need and like 1 2 3 4 5
4. I am comfortable discussing any sexual issues between us with my partner 1 2 3 4 5
5. I know my partner really appreciates me sexually 1 2 3 4 5
6. I really appreciate my partner sexually 1 2 3 4 5
7. We have satisfactorily grown and adapted to each other sexually over the years, changing as our marriage changes 1 2 3 4 5

CHAPTER FIVE

Focus: Who Talks to Whom at the Dinner Table?

Susie's story of her parents' relationship is almost shocking as she recounts it. At 47, she can barely tolerate being in the same room as them. As a child she was, by others' accounts, a 'spoiled kid'. She had clothes, toys and gizmos by the dozen. Her parents did not beat her, were not outwardly unkind to her, and ensured that she got the best of everything, from the top education to the finest grade cotton sheets on her bed. She has detested her parents all her life.

Susie recounts what dinner-time was like when she was growing up: 'We didn't have fights like some families I knew. But when I would go to eat at friends' houses, I would be astonished. The kids talked and the parents listened. The kids interrupted their parents. The parents might have been angry about this, but they let the kids talk. I never opened my mouth. What good would it have done? My parents jabbered away. They paid not a jot of attention to us. Not one jot. My abiding memory of dinner is my mother giggling. I cringe to think of it. She used to giggle at my father's stories. And he would be telling them to her just so that he could see her delight. Yucch!'

Susie's parents were absorbed in each other. They flirted with each other; each was apparently alive in the presence of the other. The children were beside the point. The main point was each other.

Does staying in love the way Susie's parents did have as its price the happiness of others – the children, most importantly? Is there an economics of love – such that it can never be equally distributed, as it was not in Susie's family, to her brother's and her cost? The other side of that coin is, of course, that the focus for the parents is not on each other, but on the children. Is the dimming of passion or love between the parents the price that must be paid? Sue and Mike, Jackie and Obi, Nina and John, would all say no, but Susie would disagree. Of the couples in this book who have managed to stay in love, the testimony shows that this is often the main struggle: keeping the focus on each other, despite children, without neglecting them. It is a main point of this book that, while this is inevitably a struggle, it is one which can be resolved in favour of both the couple and the children. As we shall see in Chapter 10, just as parents can love more than one child equally and in different ways, couples can attend to and love each other as well as their children equally and in different ways. But the danger is that because the struggle to maintain focus is so difficult, most people give it up. Most people become diverted by their love for their children. And given the difficulty described in maintaining adult love, it is all too easy to let children become the centre, and for marital love to move off to the wings.

Let us return to Susie's parents. The beam shone on each other, to the children's exclusion. In contrast, most parents concentrate on their children, to the couple's exclusion. Many of the couples in this book seem to manage to do both, at least by their own reports. Sue and Mike spend a great deal of time with their two children, now nine and six. Dinner-time is child-dominated. The children calibrate this; thrown food and tears are effective techniques for bringing focus back to them. The couple, though, makes a practice of trying to distribute focus as it is demanded between the subgroups (children and couple) of this family. Weekends see them driving the children to swimming, friends' houses and into town. But once the children are in bed, regularly by 8.00 p.m., Mike and Sue are typically together.

This brings up a robust research finding: couples who are happier together are couples who do things together and who talk to each other more[1]. This is a simple but key point. Couples who talk together might be talking about things which are trivial, and couples who spend time together may be spending time obnoxious to at least one of the partners (e.g., going to a football match, for the one, or visiting your spouse's best childhood friend, for the other).

But if you examine what is behind these findings, the link with happiness makes sense. Couples talking and spending time together and doing so *happily* are focusing on each other. And focusing on each other is likely to lead to understanding and caring about what happens, not just for yourself, but because you have understood what it means for your partner. And so when actual help, or support, or, in other words a 'protective alliance' is needed, you are more apt to provide it. This is partly because you have noticed it, as you have been focusing on your partner, and partly because you have come to care what happens to him or her. It also is likely that, through that focus, you are apt to feel that it enriches you to help your partner. It is much less likely that you will begrudge it, feel exhausted, or put upon. So the protective function – empathising, feeling for, being supportive, and giving help – is intimately connected with focus.

At various points in the life cycle focus on each other is severely tested. The couple's parents might demand attention and loyalty at the beginning of the relationship. (This is not as common as in earlier times, as young adults characteristically live apart from their parents for a time before marrying or cohabiting.) Yet first loyalty and attention may still be demanded, testing the primacy of the couple's commitment to each other. But when children arrive, as I have already pointed out, the couple's quality of focus on each other is normally shifted at least for a time on to the children. Getting it back on to each other for enough time and over a long enough period is one of the defining tasks for couples in their years of parenthood. Judging by the fall in marital satisfaction over the child-rearing years, most couples seem to fail[2]. As a couple's parents become older and frailer the focus also may go back to the family of origin. And as one or both or the couple becomes engrossed in his or her career, the focus on each other may again be severely tested. The couples who manage to retain focus on each other are not in general isolates or disloyal to others. Some, like Susie's parents, fail to achieve any balance: they preserve their love through maintaining focus at others' cost. But some, such as Sue and Mike, manage it despite struggle.

Focus and communication

Focusing is also connected to communication. Easier, clearer, more open and more direct communication, which is fundamental to all well-functioning relationships of any intimacy[3], cannot be achieved in the absence of knowledge of the other. Being in more frequent and attentive contact with your partner affords the opportunity to notice non-verbal cues about her preferences and moods, his comforts and discomforts. With the build-up of such information, greater sophistication in how to communicate with each other develops. With diminished contact between people, these skills become rusty and even outmoded as people change and develop.

What focus looks like in a relationship – what it is

Focus involves the demonstration that your partner is worthy of special attention, time and enjoyment. It means giving time and attention to your partner and indicating through choices that spending time with and energy on him/her is important. It involves sharing interests and concerns, and finding out about his/hers.

It means:

a. making time for your partner.
b. giving attention to your partner.
c. asking about your partner's concerns or showing interest in these.
d. choosing your partner to pay attention to or do things with comparative frequency over competing demands and interests such as television, music, telephone, work, hobbies, reading and, of course, other people (including children and parents).
e. attending to the importance of the content of what your partner is conveying, so that you can try to respond appropriately.
f. showing appreciation for matters of interest or concern to your partner.
g. acknowledging your partner's presence (e.g., when you have not seen each other for a while, such as when arriving home after work).
h. acknowledging your partner's feelings.
i. making time for a sexual relationship with your partner – that is, focusing your feelings of desire on your partner, showing desire, expressing appreciation of the way he/she looks and the way he/she makes you feel when you look at or touch him/her; making time for sex and also demonstrations of affection.
j. eliciting feelings, thoughts, responses and attention from your partner.

k. noticing your partner's needs, expectations and desire.
l. sharing activities, interests, thoughts and comments with your partner.
m. receiving your partner's thoughts and comments.

Focus is the opposite of neglect, ignoring, taking for granted, choosing other people and other interests regularly over your partner.

Focus as an essential element of human psychology

As attachment theorists have demonstrated, a baby is the centre of its own universe[4]. It expects its mother to be at its base, to attend to its needs, be its executor in the world. The reliability of this relationship is key to establishing a child's sense of security, power, value and faith in the reliability of the world and subsequent relationships. For the mother to successfully fulfil her role, she must be attentive and focus on her newborn, focusing almost exclusively at first, with the focus gradually diminishing as the baby becomes more self-reliant. The oft-observed phenomenon known as 'maternal preoccupation' which identifies the mother's focus on the infant describes the mother's end of the bargain. This preoccupation, or almost exclusive focus, facilitates the establishment of the child's secure relationship to her. The sense the baby has of being focused upon securely and consistently by the loved object, the fixed ally in the universe (or, the mother, at this point) forms a basic part of the experience of love. Adult lovers talk about this experience, especially at the beginning of relationships: the 'preoccupation' returns, fixed this time on the adult lover[5]. All identify this preoccupation, almost a mania, a being seized by thoughts of the lover, as a hallmark of the state of love, at least in its beginning. The condition of being in a constant state of reverie about your lover, of waiting to see and be seen by him or her, is a feature of falling in love. Also at the beginning, deep insecurity, even desperation, leading to physical symptoms such as nausea, or butterflies, or panic attacks, can engulf the lover when he/she feels the loss of focus upon him/her. These feelings mimic the state of insecure attachment in babies whose mothers are inconsistent in their quality of focusing on them, as we have remarked in Chapter 3. It would seem that focus forms a solid part of the basis of love. To ignore your partner, to take him/her for granted, to neglect him/her seriously erodes this basis. The songwriters exalt focus: 'I concentrate on you . . .' and '. . . there are thousands of stars in the sky, But they all disappear from view, For I only have eyes for you.' The banal lines reverberate; they speak a truth about love.

Other research on marital satisfaction has identified a link between the following qualities in a marriage and satisfaction: attention to each other; time spent together; interests shared; creation of a clear boundary around the couple (that is, in regard to any children, the couple's friends and relatives and parents, and also in regard to work and individual interests or hobbies), so that they do share times and interests together; and a shared sense of sexual satisfaction. All of these together constitute the quality which is superordinate to them: focus.[6]

The story of Nina and John

John and Nina, whom we first met in Chapter 3, have a relationship in which focus is perhaps the most striking element. They have been together for sixteen years. As we know, they met when John was running a nightclub near an airport and Nina, a flight attendant, visited it with a group of friends. 'It was lust at first sight,' says Nina. 'We fell in lust,' says John. Neither was looking for a serious relationship; both were already entangled with other partners. Both had already had a considerable amount of sexual experience, John having had many affairs and also a very long-term relationship, Nina having almost married someone as well as engaging in some more casual affairs.

John had never felt interested in getting married. In fact, he was cynical about relationships: 'My own parents had a rotten marriage. I certainly didn't have a very good model from them to aspire to. I really didn't treat women all that well, and wasn't really expecting to get married.' Again, this is a couple in which at least one of them had no blueprint for a happy marriage; indeed, based on his perceptions of his parents' marriage, John positively tried, during his twenties and thirties, to avoid serious commitments.

However, both knew quite soon that their own relationship posed a threat to their already established ones. Nina kept flying, which meant that in the beginning their relationship was sporadic, while John kept busy with his two nightclubs. They enjoyed each other immensely. After a few months Nina moved in; they both report they felt that '. . . we knew there was nowhere else in the world we'd rather be than right there, with each other.' But, as we have seen, the critical turning point in deepening their feelings came when Nina lost their first baby. As John said, 'That was the making of us. Any reserve I had had before left in those few weeks following that.' They married when Nina became pregnant again.

Their next trial-by-fire also turned John around. This was the premature birth of their next, surviving, daughter, her near-death experiences in her first few months and the gradual recognition that her sight would be seriously and permanently impaired. Within a few years John had sold up his business and relocated himself to the 'place in the world he most wanted to be' – home with his wife and child. He runs a new business – a charity devoted to the rights and education of the partially sighted – from their converted farmhouse, while Nina paints in her studio, a converted barn.

John's decision reflects a shift in focus, away from a business which took energy and time from his family, back to his family. 'With us it wasn't another person, or the birth of the little one, which got in the way for us, it was my business.' His clubs were thirty miles from where they lived, and demanded constant attention. In the end, one night, driving between home, hospital and business when the baby was not well, he decided that '. . . this was crazy. It wasn't worth it.' So, in time, he sold up.

There were, as for all couples, other challenges to their devotion, attention, time and loyalty to each other: from other friends and family. Perhaps because both of them had established a good deal of independence from their own families, their families were not intrusive. And because they went to live in a rather remote farmhouse the telephone became the chief source of social contact for Nina and her friends and John and his.

However, John did have to make a conscious choice with his closest friend and business partner: Nina was to come first, and this friendship did suffer for the first few years. 'But now, sixteen years later, this friend finally has a relationship which is good himself and he can understand. He also has had to admit over the years that Nina has been good for me. And now they can be friends too,' John explains, while also making clear that he was prepared to sacrifice this friendship until and unless the friend came around both to accepting Nina and also the diminution of their friendship. They have had to make their shift in priorities clear to friends and close family (such as Nina's sister, who is also a close friend); apparently, most have responded by acknowledging the sanctity of the unit.

As Nina says: 'I mean, John's my best friend so I tend to think of him and what he'd think even when I'm not with him. So my friends might confide something in me, and they will say to me, "You won't tell anybody, but I know you'll tell John." They are friends with both of us.' They consciously choose each other ahead of other friends, as Nina goes on to explain: 'Perhaps I've never been that close to my friends, in a funny sort of way. I don't need to see them a lot. If someone becomes my friend and they need an awful lot of my attention I can't give it . . . I like friends who give me space . . . and will say, you know, I don't see them for months, and they will say it doesn't matter, and we'll ring each other up and we're just the same as we were a few months ago – you know, it doesn't change. I like that sort of relationship with women. So, in a way, there's not a competition for the space with John.'

When they had a baby their intense focus could well have begun to go off-track, as great numbers of couples experience, giving almost all time and attention to their children, and eventually only relating to each other through them. Either that, or, as in the case of Susie's parents, the children get little focus upon them. Perhaps partly because of her traumatic beginnings as well, in which John and Nina, as they say, 'welded together' more fully, as a result, their daughter Lara has in effect become one more area in which they feel a joint 'project', with the difference that she has become as important in each of their lives as each is to the other. Not only have they shared the responsibilities of looking after her, they bring to each other stories, insights and concerns about her. This keeps them apprised of each other's deep feelings and information about their daughter and also ensures that she is equally a part of their lives. Again, this takes conscious choice, for it would be very easy to keep these relationships separate, not to talk about what each has talked about with the other.

Nina comments: 'She . . . makes us, I suppose, instead of two in a team, three in a team, especially as she's got older.' John elaborates: 'It's never been competitive or divisive between us as parents. From the beginning, even when I was working in the clubs I would finish work – probably leave the club at quarter to four in the morning – and get to the hospital around about five, spend three or four hours with Lara, and then come home and go to bed . . . That sort of thing started us out as equally involved with her, just dividing it up, not consciously sitting down and working out a rota, but it had to be done, and it was our responsibility and our interest to do it.' Moreover, they have built a lot of their working lives around Lara, since John began his charity for the visually impaired, which Nina also works on, increasing the range of topics on which they jointly focus.

Now the couple work and live in the same space, and, although each spends a good deal of the day engaged in his and her own pursuits, focus is shown in a multitude of ways. They come together off and on throughout the day and share what they've been thinking about and doing. For instance, when Nina was doing an art history course at a local college, John helped her with her papers. 'I'm a better typist and speller and better at grammar, so I tidy up her sentences. But I also learn something. Through her art history course I wouldn't say I've become an expert or anything like that, and I don't have her passion for art, but I've become that little bit more knowledgeable and appreciative of art because of it.' Or sometimes Nina will stop what she's doing and help John out. 'If I see that he's really busy, pushed for time, and I think there's something I can do, I just do it. Something like take a whole load of envelopes and stuff them and address them.' They find each other's projects interesting; they discuss them together in the moments when they take a break, have a coffee or tea, or just talk after dinner.

Earlier we saw that they 'read' each other; they 'know each other so well' ('John knows everything there is to know about me. He knows me better than anyone in the world. He knows when I'm upset and what makes me happy,' says Nina). They know each other through talking and noticing. They notice what the other needs, because they have consciously structured their lives so that they have the time and space in which to do so. No longer is John gone for most of the day, then exhausted for most of the evening. But living and working in the same space is not necessary to achieve this, nor does it guarantee it. Instead, it is their consciousness that they are vital to each other which underlies their focus. John chose to change his life and give more to Nina. She chooses to do the same. If either of them worked outside of the home, they could share the same quality of focus, as long as they made regular and consistent time for each other.

Their focusing results in and reveals shared humour and banter; having fun together is important to them and they create situations to give them pleasure and fun. When John has been away, as he is every so often for business, for instance, Nina makes a special occasion of his return: 'I've done the lot,' she says, 'you know, candlelit dinners, and usually I've got Lara away for the night.' Here, Nina is certainly focusing on John: in full candlelight, making an effort to make John the centre of her attention. Or, they throw theme parties, which is something which John in his club-owning years used to do, and which they had enjoyed together during that period. Every so often, they open up the barn in which Nina paints and throw something like a fancy dress or 'murder' party. Their friends might stay until the early hours. But afterwards they get the most pleasure out of doing a post-mortem together.

They profess to be as lusty together now as when they met. By focusing they are aware of the other's sexuality, to respond to it, just as to the other parts of the way in which they relate, just as the way they share their stories and comments: they take each other in, sexuality and all.

Focusing fosters intimacy. 'There's nothing we can't talk about. We talk on and on about anything,' both say. Nina elaborates: 'John's a great talker . . . even when he's away I store up things in my head – Oh, I must tell him that, I must tell him this. When he was away last week, when he came home, at ten, we actually talked until 3 a.m. . . . There are never times when I feel we've run out of things. Sometimes I've been working and I've just had to rush up to his office, because I've just got to say something to him or I'll forget it.

And it's always fun, isn't it, when you've been away for a week because you have twice as much to talk about . . . In the beginning, when I first met John and I used to fly, I used to come back and talk, and because I'd been away for, say, a week, I was really hyped up about what I'd been doing and where I'd been; every time I'd come in, John used to put the kettle on and say, "Come on, tell me about it." And that was wonderful because I'd been with other people before who . . . the last thing they wanted to do was for me to rabbit on about people they never met, or places they'd never seen. And I found that so important, that this person actually wanted to know what I'd been up to for the last week. And that hasn't stopped.'

Watching them throughout a week together, this becomes apparent. They talk about politics, art, other people, their daughter, TV and the weather, among other things. But each one does seem to be listening to the other, not distractedly doing something else. It is free and easy talk. They also play together: they have a custom of doing the crossword puzzle from the paper each day. They do it jointly, each filling in a clue, sometimes deliberately leaving a word blank so the other will have something to do. Interspersing these more protracted discussions are moments when they stop and reassure, through a teasing pat, kiss, or nuzzle, through asking, 'How are you doing?' or 'Want a cup of tea?' or 'You okay – do you need some help?' The noticing, built up through time and attention, also increases pleasure. They have a cache of comfortable in-jokes, a light and constant banter. The investment in attention and time has paid off in an increase in pleasure. They show the quality of focus in action. They show why focus is a key ingredient.

Are you putting your relationship on the back burner? Are you letting challenges to your focusing upon each other erode the quality of focus in your relationship? As you did with 'protection', it may be revealing to do this **exercise**: take the list of behaviours comprising 'focus' and assess your partner and what you think his/her assessment of you would be for this factor. Which areas would you say need work for you and your partner?

a. making time for your partner.

b. giving attention to your partner.

c. asking about your partner's concerns or showing interest in these.

d. choosing your partner to pay attention to or do things with comparative frequency over competing demands and interests such as television, music, telephone, work, hobbies, reading and, of course, other people (including children and parents).

e. attending to the importance of the content of what your partner is conveying so that you can try to respond appropriately.

f. showing appreciation for matters of interest or concern to your partner.

g. acknowledging your partner's presence (e.g., when you have not seen each other for a while, such as when arriving home after work).

h. acknowledging your partner's feelings.

i. making time for a sexual relationship with your partner – that is, focusing your feelings of desire on your partner, showing desire, expressing appreciation of the way he/she looks and the way he/she makes you feel when you look at or touch him/her; making time for sex and also demonstrations of affection.

j. eliciting feelings, thoughts, responses and attention from your partner.

k. noticing your partner's needs, expectations and desire.

l. sharing activities, interests, thoughts and comments with your partner.

m. receiving your partner's thoughts and comments.

CHAPTER SIX

Gratitude: the Demonstration of Care and Appreciation

As the psychoanalyst Melanie Klein[1] was first to emphasise, gratitude is a focal aspect of love. Between mother and infant it helps sustain the protection in love. Without it, love can be overwhelmed by destructive feelings consequent to frustration. Frustration is the experience of not getting protection or refuge which you need or expect. The other side of frustration is tremendous relief. Gratitude then flows to the one who has helped or valued you. (In the immortal pop song words of Sam and Dave: 'I didn't want to love you but I did and I do . . . And I thank you!')

The importance of expressing gratitude is more or less ritualised in every culture. In Japan, for instance, an intricate system of thanks and indebtedness shown by particular acts and gifts, exists. In comparison, we in the West have few such rituals, although birthdays, anniversaries, Valentine's Day and, to some extent, Christmas are rituals in which people show their appreciation to each other. Yet, most often, gratitude enters the lexicon of familiar complaints when it is lacking. In Mel Brooks and Carl Reiner's comedy routine of the 1960's, *The 2000-Year-Old-Man*, a man who has supposedly lived for 2,000 years is being interviewed. 'How many children have you had in all those years?' he is asked. He answers an absurdly large number and begins to enumerate his offsprings' successes and virtues and, as a parent, how hard he has worked to help them become so well-established. When he finishes he pauses for a moment, then adds, 'And not *one* of them comes to visit. Not even a postcard!'

This rueful cry, or variations on it, is on the lips of many parents of children who typically take their parents' care for granted. A different but similarly meant lament is frequently uttered by lovers: 'What thanks or appreciation do I get? He takes me for granted.'

Over time, gratitude for finding each other, commonly uttered in the early days, typically goes silent, but gratitude for emotional support and practical assistance (one the more feminine and the other the more masculine contribution) is more probably shown. The appreciation of, or gratitude given to, the lover is a part of the love experience which is often ignored. And yet it can be the transforming aspect of the relationship. Expressing gratitude means there is focus. Moreover, it implies a possibility of balance, or exchange: now that I've helped you, if I need some help, you'll give it to me. Gratitude, and its concomitant, balance, mark a clearer path on the map of future negotiations through a love relationship. And you are more likely to feel united with someone who appreciates you, and appreciation usually brings pleasure.

John and Nina report how gratitude has helped them through difficulties. John's ME has been more or less de-bilitating for a number of years: 'If Nina had acted differently I don't know how I or we would have come through this all. I really owe my recovery to her, and how she has been so sensitive to me, not to push me too far when I couldn't be, but helping me when I had the energy to do a little bit.' Do they express gratitude to each other? Does each know that the other appreciates their efforts? 'Certainly,' both reply.

Both in explicit ways and by their smiles, or nuzzles of appreciation, they have made sure each other knows.

Many couples, however, do not show gratitude. It is one of the easiest parts of loving to lose. It has been bred out of some in undemonstrative families. Others find it hard to acknowledge they need something, and expressing gratitude leaves them too exposed. In any case, without this acknowledgement, love can wither. If it is absent this means a couple consciously has to make an effort to put it into their relationship. At first awkward and stilted (in therapy, when I give people exercises to show more appreciation, to be more courteous – such as to thank each other for favours – or to acknowledge each other after absences with a kiss, I get, initially, huge resistance). As a couple changes its experience of each other, through showing real appreciation (it must be sincere to work, of course), eventually it becomes easy and habitual. They have, reciprocally, shaped each other's behaviour and replaced habits of ingratitude with ones of gratitude (as we shall describe in Chapter 12).

Tom and Kirsty had lived together for thirteen years. Their children, now nine and twelve, were their explicit reason for staying together. For ten of their thirteen years together, Tom worked in Liverpool during the week, and the family lived in Reading, where Kirsty had an administrative job. A year ago, Tom met his first girlfriend again and they began a passionate affair. He recently told Kirsty that he wanted a divorce so they could marry, but Kirsty persuaded him to have some marital therapy for the sake of the children. These sessions became the arena for Tom to regurgitate resentments and Kirsty to hurl accusations. What it boiled down to was that each felt unappreciated, Kirsty saying Tom took for granted the extent to which she had struggled to run their home, despite working, nor had he acknowledged the extent to which she had earlier in the relationship given up the fast track for Tom ('I'm not giving up another career move for you!'). Tom, meanwhile, alleged Kirsty had not appreciated that he had spent thousands of tedious hours commuting ('trying to make a decent living for you and the kids!'). He maintained that he had done his part to run their home, making a different contribution: DIY and gardening each weekend ('Do you really think after working all week and driving for hours on a Friday and early Monday morning that I seriously want to paint walls and sort out boilers?'). Years of resentment over ingratitude spewed out over a by then irrevocable divide. They played out the old chestnut, 'You take me for granted' superbly. In so doing they hastened the end of their partnership.

Couples who demonstrate appreciation do so through words, gestures, looks, acts and sometimes gifts. Iona says that Joe gives her confidence. How does he do that? In part it is: 'He's always telling me how much he loves me and how beautiful I am. He always cares about the way I look . . . and my hair, what I should wear. He buys me clothes.' Another reason Iona feels appreciated is because Joe thanks her for things she does for him. 'When he wants me to do something that I really don't want to do, but he really does want me to do it, he's got this little saying of his, he doesn't even know he does it, he goes, "Ooooh!" (like a little baby) and it just gets to me and no matter what it is, I say, "All right I'll do that," and he goes, "Will you?" and I say, "Yeah," and he'll go, "Oh, you're lovely," and put his arms round me and kiss me and I kiss him back. Just like a couple of kids really, after all this time!'

Learning to incorporate more expressions of gratitude can help turn a relationship around, as was the case with Melanie and Dave. Melanie and Dave have been married for eight years; after years of infertility they are about to become parents for the first time. Dave has a job in which he periodically has to work an overnight drive away. He arranges this in extended periods, so this has meant that the couple has experienced periodic long separations. The years of separations and infertility have left their mark; this couple speaks of the past few years as dark ones for them. However, Melanie describes how they have managed to shake that darkness and feel restored to a sense of deep and pleasurable love, and reports that one event was a turning point.

After her last infertility operation Melanie lay on her hospital bed, not daring to tempt fate by dreaming of success; doctors had warned her her chances of conception would be increased by only a small margin. She was a breath away from despair. By a grim twist of fate the operation had occurred a few days before Mother's Day and, in consequence, on Mother's Day itself she found herself, third-day-post-operatively weepy, in an Obstetrics and Gynaecology ward of a large urban hospital. Just before visiting hours, an un-familiar woman came walking towards her, bearing a single red rose. 'Hello, dear,' said the grey-haired stranger. 'We're from the Volunteers. This is to wish you a happy Mother's Day!'

Melanie, in her shock, thought a terrible joke was being played on her, until she realised that the volunteers had not been told which were the wards for new mothers and which for the rest, the non-mothers like her, the possibly never-to-be-mothers. She wept anew, in what seemed an open spigot of tears, an unending flood, and this is how Dave found her. 'What can I do for you? How can I help you?' he asked. Out of somewhere she did not know existed, she asked him to sing to her and tell her stories, which he did, and gradually he calmed her down. Later he told her he had wanted to thump someone – the hapless volunteer, the nursing sister in charge, anyone – but when he saw just how devastated Melanie was his anger receded, and he knew he had to help her.

He had learned something, but so had she. His gift melted the anger built up over his absences which had caused her to feel she had been dumped with the housework, the routine minutiae of their lives and the worry over infertility. With the meltdown she realised she had been overlooking how much Dave was in fact pitching in when he was around, although she would be critical if he put a foot wrong in what had become her domain. She understood that his job brought both security and comfort. When she thought about it, he was pretty good-natured, trying in an inefficient way to clean, cook and iron (which she had to admit he did without asking, if he spotted any items in the basket), and that she did rely on him to fix the myriad devices which always seem to break over the years (the lamps, the wonky windscreen wiper, the funny tuning on Channel 4).

'I was able to tell him how much I appreciated what he does do for me. Just doing that made him so much more open to me. And then I realised something: he had never seemed as upset as I about the possibility of not having kids. Suddenly it occurred to me that he might be afraid of his own reaction to being a father – his own biological father abandoned his mother when he was one. His mother remarried within a year, so he's always thought of his adoptive father as his only father, so much so that I had just about forgotten that fact. So I asked him about it. At first he denied it because I think he felt disloyal to his adoptive father. But then he began to talk more about it because it made sense to him, even though he'd never put words to it. He has been so into this pregnancy I can't tell you, and so protective of me and the baby! I don't know that he would have been if we hadn't had that talk, and I know we wouldn't have had it if I hadn't thanked him for what he did for me.'

The reward for Melanie – that Dave is 'into this pregnancy' – seems to her to stem directly from her appreciating and validating his contributions, letting him know how warmly supportive and protective he had been to her in ways which were about doing things for her, not, like her women friends, probing feelings. While Melanie's way of supporting him was to probe, both are ways of loving. It is to Melanie's credit that she saw that and let her husband know. Sometimes it takes a third party to make you see your partner's efforts, because daily routines tend to make us blind to them. Later, in Chapter 7, we will meet Jean and Stuart. In the midst of a downward spiral, a time of poor communication and high conflict, Stuart copied some important documents for Jean. Jean completely missed his generosity until her friends remarked on it. This prompt, which opened her eyes, was the start for them of the upward spiral, into appreciation on both sides.

Barring third parties or guardian angels to help you, you need to accept gratitude as part of the *work* in relationships. Gratitude can be one of the first things to disappear and most awkward to put back, requiring self-conscious gestures of acknowledgement, appreciation and gratefulness over everyday interactions.

What gratitude looks like in a relationship – what it is

Gratitude includes the expression or demonstration of appreciation for your partner's efforts on your behalf. It is primarily an acknowledgement, on the one hand that the efforts have been made, and on the other, when applicable, that they have provided benefit.

Gratitude can come in both direct and also indirect, verbal and non-verbal, forms. These include:
a. expressing thanks.
b. physical demonstrations of affection in response to an attempt to be helpful (hugs, kisses, pats, for example).
c. verbal acknowledgement of the effort involved (e.g., 'That must have involved a lot of time'/'That must have been really heavy').
d. expressing admiration for your partner.
e. showing delight and pride (e.g., through appreciative

107

smiles, laughs, appreciative and eager prompts to carry on holding forth).

f. admiring glances, words, nods, or smiles on the effort made or for the final product achieved (e.g., for a piece of work displayed, or for the effort gone into your partner's appearance, or for a special or difficult choice your partner has made).

g. praise for the effort, or the product, or the service performed.

h. performing a matching or contiguous act of service or effort in response.

i. giving a gift in acknowledgement.

j. agreeing to do something or perform an act which will benefit your partner, in return.

k. giving your partner compliments – e.g., on how he/she looks, on how well he/she handled a situation (particularly a difficult one between you), on his/her management of a special event, on conduct over a tricky piece of work.

The story of John and Irene

Irene, 42, and John, 43, have been married for 23 years. They have two daughters, aged seventeen and twenty. Irene suffers from arthritis, and occasionally her condition means she needs the use of a wheelchair. She is in continual pain of some kind. A few years ago, she had surgery which has helped somewhat, making the pain more bearable. John, who works for the postal service, is currently on sick leave because of an injured back which has done nerve damage to his legs. As he has been off work, and as Irene does not work, they currently spend 24 hours a day together. Instead of feeling this is too much, Irene says, in astonishment at the idea, 'Oh no! I love having him around. We can always think of something to do. We never run out of things. He is so good to me. He's always helping. We're always having a laugh. I

108

love it. I'm sorry that it has come about in the way that it has, but I think it's wonderful that we can be together all the time. There aren't enough hours in the day!'

They met on a blind date, and got engaged three weeks later. Irene was eighteen and had had a few boyfriends, John was nineteen and with very little experience of girls. Both say they felt the proverbial 'love at first sight'. However, many people feel this and the love does not develop into the lasting sort which Irene and John seem to have.

Irene's family were dead set against her marrying at such a young age and after such a brief time, but she managed to persuade them, and a few months later they married. John's parents' marriage was secure and he says it was 'happy', though he is not sure how close they felt to each other. Irene's parents' marriage was troubled. She describes her parents as distant; her father was often absent, although, she claims, a 'good man'. And her mother vented her frustrations on her children. It was not a happy household. Irene says she has no memories of her mother touching her. This is curious, because John and Irene are extremely demonstrative. While John's parents' marriage was good, Irene came unprepared by example to marriage. Again, we witness the explosion of the myth that you need to come from happy families to be happy. In this case, as in Obi's, and as we shall see in Chapter 8, Margaret and Mark's, Irene's unhappiness made her determined to correct what she had seen.

John was in the Air Force, stationed in the south of England, and Irene, who comes from Newcastle (as did John) was reluctant to leave home. She found the early years rough, missing her family and friends. John remained in the Air Force for seven years, whereupon they returned to Newcastle. During the Air Force years John was occasionally sent on missions, leaving Irene alone with their children; this was almost unbearable for them. But, as in the first few months of their relationship when John was stationed far from Newcastle, they wrote copiously. John says it was largely through these letters that he was reinforced in his first besotted feelings for Irene: 'Through her letters in the beginning I came to know her, to know her feelings, to know that she was capable of loving me, and feeling exactly like I did.'

Both speak of the tremendous sense of gratitude they have for finding each other and for the other helping to make life so rewarding: 'Personally,' says Irene, 'I think the love we have is very rare . . . John makes me happy and I try my best to make him happy, and we're very fortunate in the fact that as the years are getting on, our love has actually grown deeper.'

What she partly means by this is that she is grateful to John for changing her for the better: 'John's always been a very patient person, and I'm a lot more patient now. I have a bigger understanding than I did before I met John. John's taught me to forget about stupid things which would normally bother me – you know, to rise above it, not let it get to you.' John adds: 'I think I've become more mature through looking after Irene.'

They show each other appreciation. 'You can't improve on our relationship, really, because every day to me is a hundred per cent anyway!' Irene announces, in John's presence, and he smiles appreciatively at her. 'I always say I've got the most priceless jewels anyone will ever have – I say to John and my two girls. No amount of money can buy that happiness,' Irene reports and John concurs, 'Yes, she does say that to me.'

Irene also used to occasionally surprise John with love notes wrapped up in his lunch which he would take to work. 'These messages used to fall out at work,' John relates, laughing, 'and the blokes at work would take the mickey out of me, but at least I knew I was loved and it made me happy. The messages would say things like "I love you", "I miss you", "It was great last night" . . .' to which Irene adds, with a laugh, '. . . all night, darling!' Irene also writes John love poems, and always marks his birthday with one.

Throughout the day you see Irene and John touching,

kissing and putting their arms around each other. These, they say, also contribute to their knowledge that they are appreciated. Irene says she also knows John values her because he is so attentive to her: 'First of all,' she reports, 'everything's shared fifty-fifty all the way. John notices what needs doing, and I do, too, and we just get on with it, and do it, helping out the other. He makes me feel like I'm the only woman; he makes me feel very attractive. He seems to find no faults in me, when I know I've got loads. He doesn't tell me my faults, instead he tells me he loves me and tells me that me and the two girls are the most important things in his life.'

Neither is this one-way: 'Irene always makes sure to compliment me on the way I look; when I go out she makes sure I look smart and tells me, which I appreciate,' interjects John. 'I also know because she comes up and kisses, gives me a cuddle.' But while they find expressing their appreciation easy now, life has not been easy for them. There have been times when appreciative gestures were not so plentiful. Both have suffered poor health, and they have had severe financial problems, especially since John has been out of work.

Earlier in their marriage, Irene used to be plagued for about half the month by an extreme form of pre-menstrual tension, in which a fluid build-up caused such pressure that it made life unbearable. This was the most difficult period in their marriage. She felt so ill that the slightest sound would make her 'go mad'; she was irritable and short-fused with both John and her daughters. But according to John, 'Irene was not herself. I just knew it wasn't Irene. I knew there was something wrong. And I just wanted to get her help. I knew the true Irene would be back.' This reframing of her behaviour (see Chapter 11) saved their marriage.

During these periods Irene was not in a mind to be grateful. However, following an outburst and calming down, remorse would overwhelm her, driving her to abject apologies and avowals of gratitude for his patience and sensitivity. And during the other, good weeks of the month, she made up for her behaviour; gratitude flowed easily then. It is likely that this is what sustained John in his belief that the 'true Irene' was still there and would come back to him. Irene is deeply grateful for his forbearance, faith and patience: 'It hurts me to think about what I was like then. I would say, "Go away! I don't want to see you!" – to both the girls and John. And John would explain to the girls that it wasn't the real me talking and that the true Irene would be back, that I was not well, and he would keep them out of my way. He was just wonderful.' Eventually, her condition was diagnosed and treated, and John was proved right – the 'true Irene' came back.

John himself suffered briefly with depression, which he credits Irene for pulling him through. This occurred recently when, as a result of his injury, it became clear that he would probably not be able to return to his job: 'I had always worked. I just couldn't think what I would do. It was hard to get going in the morning. I didn't want to get washed or dressed. Irene helped by helping me do both. And if ever I wanted anything she would go and get whatever I wanted, and she just made sure I was sitting still (because of his leg problem) and just resting all the time.'

And because he was depressed and couldn't ask for help (a feature of depression), he depended on Irene's initiating overtures to him: 'She just used to try to make me laugh, and to keep me occupied . . . that helped . . . sometimes I felt really down and I wished to be left alone, but Irene just made me eventually come out of this, perked me up. She made me see it in a different way. Like the fact that we have each other, and I won't be alone at home, and we have more time with each other, and we're never lonely. I came to see she was right. So through all these things she pulled me out of the depression.' Moreover, eventually, when his depression lifted John experienced his full range of emotions and could express his gratitude to Irene again. It is likely that this is what sustained Irene in her belief that she, too, would get her old

John back. 'I told her that I love her, and what a good life I've got, and I'm just grateful for her being there – I say that any time, really, but I did tell her then,' explains John.

They say that they are reassured 'that we still have the love for each other' through stroking each other, as they sit together on the sofa, or when embracing, or giving each other pecks of affection. These gestures of appreciation reinforce their relationship. Watching them throughout their day you see plenty of evidence of this. John frequently soothes Irene's arthritis by massaging her feet and hands. She lies flat on the sofa, closes her eyes and looks serene, taking in the pleasure and comfort he gives her. She murmurs an appreciation. Irene comes in with the shopping, which John immediately starts to help put away. They give each other a peck on the cheek; John touches her arm and calls her 'pet', affectionately. Later they nuzzle each other as they sit at the kitchen table. They smile often at each other, laugh uproariously at each other's jokes. As one talks the other gazes back with immense delight and affection. Later still, Irene, ready for bed, finds John asleep on the sofa. 'Hello, pet,' he says; she goes over to nuzzle him, lets him know that she wants to help him get up and into bed; he thanks her, kisses her; they cuddle together on the sofa.

The free and easy expression of gratitude, the demonstration of appreciation and affection that this couple shows provides the ground for the easy flow of pleasure so evident between them. Their lives are not easy, marked by physical pain and economic distress as they are, but there is no show of misery or deprivation between them. Quite the opposite.

The following **exercise** is to get you thinking about the expression of gratitude in your relationship. As with protection and focus, assessing your partner, and what you think is his or her view of *you* on the factor of gratitude, may be revealing. How satisfied are you with your partner? And how satisfied do you think he or she is with you about the following:

a. expressing thanks.

b. physical demonstrations of affection in response to an attempt to be helpful (hugs, kisses, pats, for example).

c. verbal acknowledgement of the effort involved (e.g., 'That must have involved a lot of time', 'That must have been really heavy').

d. expressing admiration for your partner.

e. showing delight and pride (e.g., through appreciative smiles, laughs, appreciative and eager prompts to carry on holding forth).

f. admiring glances, words, nods, or smiles on the effort made or for the final product achieved (e.g., for a piece of work displayed, or for the effort gone into your partner's appearance, or for a special or difficult choice your partner has made).

g. praise for effort, or the product, or the service performed.

h. performing a matching or contiguous act of service or effort in response.

i. giving a gift in acknowledgement.

j. agreeing to do something or perform an act which will benefit your partner, in return.

k. giving your partner compliments – e.g., on how he or she looks, on how well he/she handled a situation (particularly a difficult one between you), on his/her management of a special event or on conduct over a tricky piece of work.

CHAPTER SEVEN

Balance: the Give and Take in a Relationship

Joe, 54, and Iona, 49, have been married for 31 years. They live in a small bungalow with their younger son, Ian, sixteen. Joe has a furniture-making business, while Iona is a freelance hairdresser. In many ways their relationship is traditional, with Joe being the primary breadwinner, and Iona mainly looking after the home. But because of the way they look after each other the reality is not rigid.

'When Joe had a factory and there were lots of orders and lots of work to do I would go and work on the factory floor,' says Iona. Joe says, 'I don't really think it's right for a woman to get her hands dirty, to do that kind of work. But when I needed the help, Iona just pitched in and did it.' By the same token, Joe helps Iona with the house. 'I'm not a very good cook, but if I think that Iona's tired I'll just take over. I'll fold her clothes and put them away, or if I see the floor needs doing and I've noticed she's tired or very busy, I'll just get down and do it myself.' Iona says, 'He's very good about helping me with things – we always do the dishes together; he helps me out ever so much.' Watching them through the week you see them at the sink, one of them washing, the other drying, as they entertain each other with stories and jokes.

'Iona makes me feel happy. She's so nice and good and

cheerful. She looks after me and our children really well. She makes me feel so good. She makes it feel like the sun is shining,' says Joe.

'Joe gives me confidence. "You can do anything," he says. He gives me security. He's always there. He worries about my safety and he would be in there fighting if I needed it,' says Iona. Each can say what the other gives, and each feels it is evenly balanced.

The other side of gratitude is *balance*, or, a reciprocity of both effort and concern. People eventually become drained and exploited when it is one-sided. Give and take, say the songs ('please love me as I love you' is the bottom line of most). There must be a balance, warn the novels and films of doomed love, with women walking out on undemonstrative and exploitative husbands (as, for instance, Sue Kaufmann's 1960s novel, *The Diary of a Mad Housewife*, made into a Hollywood movie; or as in the film *Thelma and Louise*). In a slanging match about relationships the worst a woman can be called (by another woman) at this point in history seems to be a doormat; a man, a wimp (by another man). Both describe states of exploitation or unreciprocated concern.

Psychoanalyst Melanie Klein[1] discussed the need for some balance even between mother and infant, for the mother to be replenished enough to nurture her baby properly. Otherwise her own exhaustion (and even rage and envy, says Klein, for what the baby is getting) overwhelms her. The American psychoanalyst, Therese Benedek, in an important article on pregnancy and the early stages of motherhood[2] also describes how important it is to receive affirmation from your baby. It engenders the equilibrium which you can easily lose in the demanding early days of motherhood (when, says Benedek, you reproduce your own infantile experience, if now from the other point of view). This is one reason new parents breathe a sign of relief when their newborn finally smiles at them. The sense of gratification returned – you do have a baby who takes pleasure in you! – is intoxicating. Some return for the love you give feeds your experience of love.

Joe and Iona show an equity of gratitude, protection, focus and pleasure. In most cases the enactment of these work dynamically: that is, particularly when they are marked (through gratitude) they breed your partner's will to reciprocity. What he or she reciprocates with, however, may not be in kind.

For example, when at 45 Judith underwent a mastectomy, her husband Robert not only took over her domestic responsibilities during her long months of recovery, he learned all he could about her disease and its treatment. As a scientist, he helped interpret the information she was given in her numerous hospital visits. He fielded phone calls. He listened to her for hours, and held her when she sobbed in fear.

Fortunately, Robert has never had to suffer in quite the same naked and direct way, as he himself has been remarkably healthy. So when Judith recovered she returned his efforts in a different way. Robert depends on Judith: her diplomacy and vast reserves of energy and hospitality help defuse a potentially explosive relationship with his sickly and demanding parents. He feels awkward in groups, while gregarious Judith eases the way for him. ('We rehearse the cast list before we leave. I brief him on who will be there and what he can expect, so he is not thrown. I don't quite – but almost – hold his hand; I anxiously watch him until he seems relaxed.')

Balance is as important as gratitude. For in the cases in which it is not engendered, the giving partner becomes resentful, angry, depleted, diminished and even depressed.

What balance looks like

A basic problem emerges in portraying balance. For, as we have seen in Chapter 1 and will elaborate on further in Chapter 11, men and women typically express their love differently. To recapitulate, as research by the American researcher Francisco Cancian[3] has shown, men typically show love through practical help, financial support and sexual desire, while women tend to measure love through the exchange of talk, in particular, intimate talk and affection, which does not necessarily lead to (nor does it, however, necessarily exclude!) intercourse.

What is balance within a couple, then? This is the conundrum which the largely feminine construction of love lands us in. Successful heterosexual couples are able to decode their partners' gestures of love, so the women appreciate typically male gestures, and vice versa. The key is that they make the partner aware of their appreciation, which is why gratitude and balance are so intimately linked. Without it, it would be difficult for a man to know that his partner recognises his efforts or for a woman to know that her husband has seen that talking is not just noise but intimacy. As John Gray's catchy book title says, 'Men are from Mars, Women are from Venus'[4]. The two different species need to cross the divide quite explicitly to know they've got through to each other.

Jean and Stuart, who are two professionals in their early thirties, had almost parted when they learned this lesson about balance. Each was failing to recognise what the other was giving, according to his and her own lights. They saw what was not happening, rather than what was. Shortly after their marriage, Jean left Stuart for two months to nurse her ill mother, leaving him alone in an alien city and starting a new job. Jean's persistent failure to focus on him (choosing instead her parents) drove Stuart away. This crucial failure initiated a downward spiral, but it was kept going by their mutual failure to appreciate the efforts which were being made to keep them together.

A few months into the downward spiral they visited friends for the weekend. The weekend preceded a major presentation at Jean's work. On the Sunday she suddenly realised that she was short of accompanying fact sheets and reference lists. In a panic she drew everyone into her crisis. No copy machines could be located easily on a Sunday, but Stuart managed to find a cooperative friend at a not distant university who would make his machine available. He drove the distance, made copies and bound the report; moreover, unbidden, he adjusted the title page, which was slightly off-centre.

The context for the crisis was, however, months of sexual and emotional warfare. While Jean, out of guilt, consistently made sexual overtures, Stuart generally rebuffed them. Their daily exchanges turned into sniping matches. Jean felt so angry at Stuart that she was blind to his generosity that weekend. When he returned she picked an argument with him over a small detail of the binding. 'Wait a minute,' interjected their hosts, 'while Stuart may have been a sod all these months, what was he doing for you today? Who looked at your work and cared enough to make it even better?' Jean, disarmed and humbled, ammunition gone, apologised and expressed her thanks. This was the start of an upward spiral and the couple remained together, eventually much more happily.

People sense a balance, overall, in their relationships if efforts and concern for each other are indeed reciprocal. Usually balance flows along with gratitude.

Jackie talks about how she and Obi exchange periods of looking after their daughter Atalanta and running the household when the other one needs a break: 'I mean, sometimes I'll say, "Look, I don't want to see you, I don't want to see Atalanta. I just want to go upstairs, on my own and be there for five or ten minutes." And Obi will say, "Okay, fair enough. I'll hold on to Atalanta for you." . . . But then I will do it for him. In fact, he's actually studying for exams at the moment, and he will say, "Jackie, I'm working upstairs, can you make sure Atalanta doesn't come upstairs" . . . because as soon as she finds out that her dad's gone she will trundle upstairs, so I have to keep her busy. And on Saturdays he goes to the library so I look after her predominantly on a Saturday . . . It's a partnership. He sacrificed a lot for me this year because I've given up my job to do my teacher training . . .

(even though) he does worry financially . . . But then I said to him, "I promise, whatever happens, I will get a job at the end of the course." ' That reassured Obi, and achieved balance to his sacrifice. In fact, Jackie had just secured a job for the following year at the time of her interview for this book.

Donna and Steve had been married for sixteen years, with two sons, when Donna's feelings of exploitation drove her to divorce. It was not just that she had discovered, over the years, evidence of four affairs. (In fact, she herself had had two retaliatory ones.) Steve's last affair had certainly made her feel less inclined to forgive and forget, but what she was seeking from Steve was not so much assurance of fidelity (he could come up with promises by the armfuls) but rather, as she says, 'a demonstration that he was able to think about me, to respond to my need for . . . support.'

'All these years I've had to think about you, Steve,' she cried, as they discussed her decision to leave. 'I've had to make it all right for you, make sure that you feel secure, give you a good home, look after your kids, do all the running involved with them, talk to you when you've been down, make you feel better. When you hurt me, I have had to try to understand and to make you feel better because you feel so guilty and are so afraid of losing me. But what about me? Where's the interest in things I like? You have stopped me from having other friends or developing my talents. You have asked me to stop my university course because you are so afraid I'll become too involved with the other students.' Donna went on and on, describing more ways Steve's life has carried on, unimpeded, with no regard for her. 'When have you ever lifted a finger in this house, gone to a school meeting, tried to talk to your sons or to me or to get to know my friends, while I have had to socialise with your work cronies and throw parties for them whenever you want them?' Steve listened to this litany and had no comeback. 'You're right, Donna,' he said. 'But I love you.'

Clearly, for Donna, the balance, the reciprocity, of love

was lacking, and after sixteen years of it she no longer loved Steve. It was the erosion of her feelings under the steady drip of her unreciprocated nurturance of their relationship which made it possible for Donna to leave. Lack of balance can kill in just this way.

Joe and Iona's story

Joe and Iona grew up in the same part of the East End of London. Iona had once noticed Joe at a pub when she was sixteen and he was twenty. She was attracted to him, but nothing happened; he didn't seem to notice her – perhaps she was too young. The next summer they both happened to be staying at the same seaside town for their holidays. Joe noticed her then: after seeing her on the beach, he manoeuvred it so that he and his friend took out Iona and one of her friends. They have been together ever since, marrying when Iona was one month short of her eighteenth birthday. 'Most of the friends we had who got married then are divorced. We look at ourselves and think how lucky we are,' says Iona with a wide, disingenuous smile.

But it has not been clean sailing. 'Those early years were really rough,' says Joe, shaking his head at the memory. 'Two horrible rooms, no indoor toilet, damp and cold. It wasn't a fit place for my wife. I feel Iona's really, you know, like a lady, at least those are my feelings about her. I didn't want her to have to live like that. It just wasn't right.' But Joe was proud and wanted to provide for himself, even though his own parents had some money they could have lent them. He started up a furniture-making business with a partner and slowly but surely began to make a more comfortable living. But during those early rough years there were frequent rows. 'Joe has a really quick temper,' says Iona. 'It's better now, but it was bad in those days.'

Joe explains, 'I was indulged, spoiled as a boy. I was used to getting what I wanted right away. I wasn't patient

121

in those days. I had to learn and it took a long time.'

They both had to learn. Iona comments that she learned to understand his quick temper. 'I knew he didn't mean it. I knew he would get over it and come back and feel really bad.' As we saw in Chapter 4, they learned a way of dealing with these rows which they still use today.

However, the rows erupted badly when their older son was 28 and still living at home. As Iona reported in Chapter 4 this was a time when Joe and she considered splitting, although within days the break was mended and they eventually found a solution to their problems, both their son's inability to leave home and also the frequency of Joe's outbursts.

As we saw, Joe and Iona have fairly traditional male and female roles within their family. Joe has been the main breadwinner and Iona has looked after the children and their domestic life. Each says that the other's contribution to the family's welfare has been well appreciated. (Joe has been a good provider and helped to make them feel secure and protected, according to Iona, and Iona has been the model mother, a wonderful cook and efficient keeper of the home, according to Joe). These roles have overlapped at various times, such as when Iona had to earn extra money when employment was scarce, or when Joe had to look after their small son when Iona was in hospital after an ectopic pregnancy. But as their children have grown up and over their 31 years together, Joe and Iona have also learned to cross over into each other's domains, in the name of helping the other. Over the years, they have developed a remarkable ability to give and take from each other. Iona describes this in the following:

'If I get behind in what I'm doing, like just one of the things he might do - say the floor needs washing, and what with the dog going in and out it gets really muddy - and I'm busy, and I say, "Oh, Joe, you know that floor's really bothering me, I must wash that tonight," and if he gets in before me it'll be washed. He'll say, "I've done the floor – you don't have to worry!" And if there are big piles of ironing, I mean, he had never ironed in his life before, but lately the ironing's piling up (I try to do like a half hour here and there). I came in one day and he says, "I've done the ironing (mind you it was awful, it was terrible – but he's got much better). And I said, "Oh! That's wonderful, Joe!" And he puts it all away; he never leaves it in a pile. All the time he's helping me . . . Those sorts of things, all the time. We work together and the longer we've been married the better it is in that way. For instance, he's no gardener, but I love the garden; he cuts the grass and he's tried, sort of, doing the edges, but he doesn't know a weed from a flower, you know, so he cuts it all down. But he'll sort of go around and say, "Oh, I've done this," and I go around and I think "Oh! He's chopped all the flowers down, you know!" But I say, "Oh, it's lovely, Joe, that's really nice, but perhaps you shouldn't do that bit again!" But in every way to do with the home he's trying to help me.'

Iona recognises that she does things just for Joe, as well: 'If there's some particular meal he wants and says, "Oh, I really fancy that!" I cook it for him . . . Or, he likes a really casual kind of holiday, while I really like staying in hotels and being waited on. But that makes him uncomfortable. We've been to a few hotels and I can tell he's not happy. He loves caravans; that's why we've got a caravan. It doesn't necessarily mean me cooking on holiday, but he likes it if I do, and I don't mind. For his sake I have the casual holiday.' Another example of this kind of give and take is when they are shopping – each one is thinking of the other and what he or she might need or want. So Joe often buys Iona clothing or perfume and Iona buys Joe things such as special shower gel that he might like.

'Not long ago,' relates Iona, 'when I went shopping I didn't have an awful lot of money. But as we both do aerobics we both use a lot of shower gel - tons of it - and we had run out. Since I didn't have a lot of money I couldn't buy some for both of us (we use different kinds). So I bought Joe some shower gel that he likes. I just used soap.'

But in some couples doing things for their partner feels like a burden. Iona and Joe do not feel this because, as Iona puts it, 'I know that if I ever want Joe to do something for me he will do it, so I do things for him when he asks me . . . I know that if ever I needed Joe to do something for me he would. He would just do it. We give and take, and it's become second nature now. We don't even think about it.' It is this longer perspective, which reminds the individuals of the partnership and interdependence, the cornerstone of protective love, which keeps the balance going.

Joe comments that Iona is always doing things for him, from the mundane to the unusual. '. . . Iona's always there when I come back from work. And when's she's there it feels like the light's switched on. I hate it when she's not there. And she's always got food on the table and the house in order. I do loads of washing up – I'm always washing up. And if Iona's busy and she can't do certain things around the house I do it for her . . . She doesn't need to ask me, like about washing the dishes. I know she's stood at the stove and cooked. But sometimes we ask each other to do things. We always do it for the other if we can . . . By helping one another through each day, you know, things are good. It helps you to put a smile on it. And we tell each other our innermost thoughts. It's nice to be able to tell your wife your innermost thoughts and your weaknesses, because men like the macho thing, you know. We don't cry and we're not supposed to have weaknesses, but I've always felt that I can talk to Iona about things. And she talks to me. It's nice that I can always go to her when I'm down, and she can come to me.' He reiterates: 'Iona makes me happy . . . When I come home and she is here it's like the house is filled with sunshine,' says Joe unaffectedly, with great feeling.

Iona says, 'Joe gives me protection. I always feel safe with him around. He is always thinking about my security and safety. He believes in me. Whatever, he says, "You can do that!" I know he is always thinking about me and whether I'm all right or need anything.' She grows pensive when asked about the time she thought about leaving him. 'I couldn't have done it. I thought about him moving away and I knew it just wasn't possible.' She stops and grows quiet and then says, 'I'd have died. I'd die without him.' She is quiet for a moment then a huge smile beams across her face as she thinks about what that means – how much they love each other.

As an **exercise**, take a moment to see how you rate yourself, or how your partner would rate you, right now, on the factor of 'balance'. Think of two other couples, one with a marriage in which you think there is a definite imbalance of effort (that is, one partner in the couple makes all the running). Then think of one in which you would say there is a pretty even balance. Where would you say your partner would put you in relation to these two couples? Why (that is, what is his or her reasoning, suspending your judgement for the moment on its validity)? Where would you put yourselves and why? Have you and your partner discussed your *respective* feelings about who seems at the moment to be putting more into the relationship? Next, name one thing you think your partner would like you to do to redress the balance, and one thing you think you might be able to do.

CHAPTER EIGHT

Pleasure

In the discussion so far there may have been an implication that gratitude, focus, balance and protection are given pleasurably. There are couples who look as if they are exchanging help and services, but do so out of resentment and competition. This tit for tat mentality operates when doing things *for* each other as often as against. Similarly, there are couples who do focus on each other, but often at others' cost, and the focus is unpleasant or unwillingly given.

For example, Dan and Cathy have been married for ten years; they have two small daughters. Dan is in the military while Cathy is a part-time social worker. Because of Dan's job they have moved every few years since their marriage. They are very efficient at these dislocations and transplant-ations. With precision honed by the military they pick up stakes and put them down again, depending on a rota dictating who does what and when. Their lives are recorded in rotas and calendars; the calendar documents their schedules and social obligations – for example, Sundays are designated 'Family Days'. As a result, their domestic life looks a smooth partnership, with few arguments.

However, Cathy says, 'I never get the feeling that Dan wants to do something just for me or wants just to be with me; that he gets pleasure out of doing things because I would enjoy them. I think he stays with me out of duty.' But Cathy also admits that there is a competition for who is the 'better' spouse or parent. 'He could never complain that I don't look after his house and kids. I am the model wife and mother, in our friends' eyes. I can't let anything slip or I'll be the guilty one – I always think he's judging me and I'm falling short. Some of it is that he is such a workaholic. He has the puritan ethic down to an art form, so that if I'm sitting down, relaxing, I get very conscious of him buzzing around working, and I think I'm being slothful.'

It may just as well work the other way, too, for Dan says much the same. 'We never relax; it is true that if I see her reading the newspaper while I'm working I get irritated, but the same is true of her, if she sees me listening to music.'

This couple is so highly regimented and competitive that their life looks as though it is one of smoothly running give and take, when in fact it is straitjacketed out of pleasure. Many couples negotiate in a tit for tat way. They keep tallies of everything done and expect something in return. And things may be given in return simply because it is clear that a tally is being kept. No one wants to be accused of selfishness, and everyone wants a chance for sainthood. This is not the kind of balance happy couples display. Many couples spend all of their time together, or neglect other relationships in favour of being with each other. A sense of obligation or fear or a need to convince the partner of loyalty may be driving these expressions of focus. Again, this is not the kind the happy couples characteristically display.

Cathy and Dan also spend much of their time together. Part of that is Cathy's terror of being alone. Very infrequently, Dan's job necessarily takes him away, but for the most part he has managed to keep these trips to a minimum. His career has suffered, as he has had to take safe jobs, declining the more glamorous, demanding ones which would send him on far-off missions (which was his reason for joining the military in the first place). He describes his career history as a matter of choice, but he betrays resentment and duty as he does so: 'I sometimes get very upset when I watch others get promoted around me and I realise that Cathy doesn't understand how much I have given up for her. I don't really enjoy my job. It's not what I joined the military for – to push paper – but I know I can make a good, honest living this way, and it suits my family life. But I do know other families who make it through with the men going away. I gave that up.'

When marriage becomes a trap filled with responsibility and unwelcome demands for attention, love suffers. When it is an experience of pleasure it grows. The descriptions of balance, focus and protection given in the previous chapters are descriptions of pleasurable experiences or ones which breed pleasure between the couple.

Joe and Iona say that a large part of their pleasure derives from the quiet companionship each gives the other. This sense of comfort and security underpins the rest of their enjoyment. 'Life would be . . .' starts Iona. 'Very dull without each other,' finishes Joe, and Iona adds, 'Pointless, a bit pointless to be honest . . . It *would* be very dull. I don't know why I'd be doing things . . . You know, day-to-day life *would* be very dull and pointless . . . I think the longer you've been married . . . the happier you become, don't you?' To which Joe answers, 'Yeah, the more contented.'

Margaret, who is a 42-year-old mother of two sons, and who has been with her husband, Mark, for twenty years, says that the most pleasurable thing about being with him is that 'I think it's just . . . we're so comfortable together. We don't have to pretend to be anybody we're not. We don't have to try and impress each other. We see each other at the best, we see each other at the worst . . . there are no secrets; we can talk about anything.'

Part of the secret happy couples have found to maintaining a high degree of interest and enjoyment between each other is that they are open to doing things, that they find things to do together or separately, and if separate, they share these by talking about them. According to Joe, 'We still try and make it interesting all the time. So all these new things that are happening, we try and make happen for one another. I suppose it makes the longing to be with each other that much more needed.'

'You have to keep trying,' says Iona, '. . . to keep your life from getting dull. You can't be lazy . . . You know, often I can't be bothered to do a certain thing . . . but after, I'm really pleased I've done it.' She talks about fighting inertia because, again, in a longer-term perspective of a partnership, this will enhance it. 'The same with me' says Joe. So Joe and Iona are often trying new activities, such as the aerobics class they take together, or getting themselves mobilised to take walks together, weather permitting or not. 'You know, going some-where – sometimes I think, I don't really want to go, I'd much rather stay here, stay at home today. Then I think, no, we will go, and I end up being really pleased . . .' and Joe finishes her sentence '. . . that we've gone. But we're always trying to fit new experiences into our lives to make it more interest-ing. Both together and separately.'

And when couples do do things separately they take pleasure in talking about these to their partners. As Nina said, it was such a pleasure for her to come back after her flying trips and tell John all about the people and places she had just experienced, and it made her feel special that this person was so interested. Or, as Jackie reports, 'Because you like each other, you make the time. Like for sex, even though with a child there's less time, you make the time, like if you know she's going to get up at a certain time in the morning, you get up a bit earlier. You have to make the time for each other.' Jackie, as well as Joe and Iona, is bringing in here the fact that pleasure can die if it is not tended. It takes a conscious effort – again, part of what is meant by working at a relation-ship.

Or, when Mark goes off to work and returns, he and Margaret will sit and talk about his day and hers, catch up on things together. Margaret says, 'If there's only two of us in the house sometimes we sit quietly; Mark will read the paper, I will read a book. But even then something will come out; you know he might say something to me, and I'll give him a reply, and that starts us off, you know . . .' Mark says that one of the most enjoyable aspects of their relationship is the fact that '. . . we always know that there will be something to say.'

As Mark works shifts, there are some days in which they find quite a bit of time together, unencumbered by children. During these hours they might play cards, or go for a drive and a walk on the beach, they might call on one of Margaret's relatives who lives nearby or entertain instead in their own house, go shopping, or potter about the house each doing something (Mark irons, Margaret cooks, for example), taking breaks for cups of coffee or tea brought to each other. This is making time for pleasure. Sharing activities and interests is a source of pleasure for them, as it is for most couples. As Iona and Joe pointed out earlier, 'You have to make the effort to keep things interesting, to keep trying new things.'

Mark expresses the pleasure this couple gets from feeling comfortable together as well as reciprocally cared for when he describes how they take pleasure in knowing that 'We'll just be doing things for each other: I'll do a spot of ironing, I know that Margaret will be thinking of me when she cooks – she's a good cook and cooks things with me in mind – and we'll take each other a cup of tea and then we might have a game of cards or something.' It is just comfortable and secure, and this is part of what Mark means by the pleasure he takes in his marriage.

Another aspect of pleasure is the delight which can come from expressed gratitude. Irene and John find it very easy to tell each other how much they love each other, and find it very hard to pass each other without touching. These serve as reminders '. . . just that she loves me,' says John, and Irene says that there are ways she knows that John loves her too.

Pleasure in each other is something which emanates from the combination of the other factors. Feeling a sense of protection, which breeds comfort and security (as Margaret pointed out above); being focused upon, which means sharing time, attention and interests (as Joe and Iona and Nina and John have related; feeling appreciated and appreciating your partner (as Irene and John discussed); and doing things for your lover and having things done for you in return (as Mark and Margaret indicated) form part of the deep pleasure these couples express.

Sharing a sense of humour is perhaps the most obvious sign of pleasure you observe in happy couples. They show delight in each other and make each other laugh. This can be seen through gentle joshing or in the stream of one-liners and steady banter that Margaret and Mark display. This kind of joking characterises Margaret's family and it was something Mark eventually learned. As he says, 'In the family I came from, I dare say, there wasn't a lot of laughter . . . Looking back on it, I see that I had to adapt to it; this was a whole new environment, with Margaret being so vivacious and open and forthright . . . my eyes just went wide open and I thought, well, I really enjoy this! I'm going to stay here; I'm going to stay here for as long as I can – and I'm still here!' Mark was undaunted by the work that lay ahead of him – that is, to develop a rapid-fire humour that matched Margaret's. This effort, with the perspective of partnership, was one worth making. Margaret corroborates this, saying that Mark learned quickly, from 'having no sense of humour . . . I had to explain "that's just a joke!"' to being 'the person in the world who makes me laugh the most.'

Mark reports that 'the laughter is more or less continual, if you like, from first thing in the morning to last thing at night . . . If you make a mistake, you have a laugh about it and you put that mistake right, or try to put that mistake right.' And when there is a conflict, or an argument, humour is part of the process of healing. 'Humour comes in straight away,' says Mark when such things occur. Margaret may get into a huff, but soon, after taking time out, thinking about it first from her point of view, then from Mark's, and then cooling down, she comes back in and they return to laughing and making a joke together. 'Oh,' says Mark, 'we go on about, like sort of hitting each other (in jest) and patting each other, or tapping each other, something like that, or a tickle here and there, just to sort of you know, start to boost yourself back up again and realise that, hey, come on, let's forget about it, let's get on . . . it's not worth it in the long run.'

The way back to loving feelings is through humour and reassurance. Along with the jokes come smiles, hugs, atonement ('I've been silly,' as Mark says, or, 'It's not so important,' as Iona says). This increases the upward slope towards pleasure.

Sharing a sense of humour is something which is usually first spotted in a nascent state. Couples develop their own form of wordplay and banter. So John and Nina pretend that Nina is oversexed and John can't keep up with her, or Margaret jokes with Mark about his long-ish nose ('When he bumps into things we blame it on his nose'), while Mark joked with Margaret about her weight a few years ago when she had put too much on ('What are you looking at?' Margaret says she asked Mark one day, when he was gazing at her romantically. 'Oh, darling, it's just that I was marvelling at how I love a woman with two butts' – and the two roared with laughter at this). It is developed, like a special language between each other, referring to particular events or characteristics they have shared on the one hand and learned about each other on the other.

And a shared sense of humour is something which can add to the sexual frisson between the couple. Mark and Margaret's banter skirts the edges of danger, so there is an excitement which makes it like flirting. It keeps them on their toes. When asked if they still look at each other and think, 'Oh boy!' Mark readily says, 'I do!' To which Margaret quickly replies, 'She doesn't mean when you're looking in the mirror, Mark. She means when you're looking at me.' Mark then answers, turning to Margaret, 'I do, because I'm just fascinated by you.' Margaret then admits that, 'I can still look at him and get, you know . . .' and then she laughs throatily. And the sexual frisson means sexual pleasure. Contrary to what most people think, these long-married happy couples claim that sex gets better over their years together, although it is no longer the urgent release of hungry passion.

Margaret explains: 'You have more time for each other as you get older, because your children don't need the kind of care they did before . . . So once our bedroom door is shut then the bedroom door is shut until the following morning . . . You can take your time. There's no urgency about it.' Mark picks up the thread: 'As Margaret says, we've got more time for each other . . . And it comes back to . . . it doesn't have to be a regular thing. It's part of our life.' And Irene says, 'It's not as often, but the quality's better. I say, roll on when he's sixty – it's like wine, it gets better with age!' To which John adds, enthusiastically, 'Definitely . . . believe me.' Irene continues: 'The lust goes, but a passion, when you are "making love", not "having sex", comes in . . . We feel passionate about each other. Sex doesn't happen as often, but when it does, it's better.'

Sex often grows out of the secure and easy display of affection throughout the day. 'Sex is not something which just happens in bed. It's going on all day, through the loving gestures and the words, and the good feelings. You don't have to end up in bed together. It goes on, building up throughout the days.'

Joe and Iona, like the others, often banter pleasantly throughout the day, punctuating their day with affectionate gestures, reassuring each other through gentle nuzzles, hugs, kisses and pats. As Irene says, this is part of the sexual story, even if these are not explicit sexual signals. All of the couples report that frequency of sex diminishes over the years, but not satisfaction.

Joe says, 'We've never had a problem with sex. Never. I've always been adventurous and Iona has always gone along with it, to a point.' The courage to go along with it is partly out of and also adds to a sense of security within this couple. 'I don't put any pressure on Iona at all.' But they put sex into a perspective. 'I don't think sex is the be-all and end-all,' says Iona, 'and if you take it lightly, I think it can be wonderful, sex.'

Knowing each other better makes it easier for these couples to please each other. 'I always try to please Iona in every way. I'm thinking of her. And there's give and take in our sexual relationship,' says Joe.

But this give and take, this mutual pleasing, takes time to work out. Irene says that John knows her so well that he knows how to please her now, and she him. While at first they felt deeply lustful for each other, they might not have known exactly what would remain pleasing over time. But during the years, they have explored each other's bodies and now know what is and is not pleasing to each other. This is the kind of sexual pleasure which grows with time. But it does demand patience and the perspective that we have time together; gratification does not have to be automatic and immediate.

The story of Margaret and Mark

Margaret, 42, and Mark, 38, like John and Irene, met when they were young and, according to both of them, 'fell in love at first sight'. In fact, Margaret had drifted into an engagement with a boy she had been dating, and was engaged at the time she met Mark in a nightclub. 'I broke the engagement off three days later,' reports Margaret. 'It was obvious I didn't feel about my then boyfriend anything like what I felt about Mark.'

But Mark, it turned out, was four years younger than Margaret. In fact, he was so young, that, being three days short of his eighteenth birthday he was in the nightclub illegally. But instead of feeling that this would be an obstacle, Margaret saw the humorous side, from the beginning. 'He was my toyboy, that's all!' And they started as they went on, with humour and delight dominating.

'I'm from Liverpool. I was in the Navy, playing football for the Navy, and on a football tour. I'd joined to have adventures, see the world – I never pictured myself settling down at that point – and we were in Newcastle. My friend who was from Newcastle took me to this club where we met these girls. He went to introduce me to them, saying, "This is Scouse" (which was my nickname in the Navy). And this girl says, "Oh, are you Scottish?" I cracked up. And when I explained to Margaret that "Scouse" meant Liverpool not Scotland, she just cracked up too.' In other words, they both saw from the outset the humorous side of things first. And this is probably their strongest bond – the ability to laugh together and take delight in things together.

Both describe an immediate physical attraction. 'It was like a thunderbolt,' says Mark. 'It was lust at first sight,' says Margaret. 'I still feel turned on by Margaret all the time,' confesses Mark. Margaret agrees, 'Yes, it's still a great thing between us.'

Margaret was in the WRAF stationed in Newcastle at the time they met, while Mark, in the Navy, was at sea much of the time. They wrote letters, and both talk of the heartache of being apart.

'We had got on like a house on fire... Being separated then was terrible. It's hard to put it into words. I just wanted more. You know, I mean, if we were walking down the street and we were holding hands, that wasn't enough, you know. He would have to put his arm around me and sort of cuddle close – then I felt closer to him. And when he wasn't there it was as if everything was suddenly boring. You know, all the things I used to do before were quite boring because Mark wasn't there. It was like a physical pain – you know, you just wanted to be with each other. It was like you weren't complete. You just had to be near each other, touch each other. I just wasn't happy unless I was with him, holding him!' Margaret reports, her eyes wide and the passion of her feelings still palpable.

Early on in the relationship, however, there were problems which threatened to undermine their alliance. Jealousy and insecurity were recurrent themes. Margaret was used to doing her own things, especially as she was still living where she had friends and family. She wanted to see them. But Mark did not want her out of his sight. They struggled with this, until Mark came to accept that this '. . . was Margaret. This was who she was'. But he could not have come to this if Margaret had not realised that '. . . he needed reassurance. That I loved him and wasn't interested in anyone else, but that we didn't own each other. Eventually he started doing his own things, too, like playing football.' Each made an effort to understand what the other needed. It became a non-issue, as Mark learned about Margaret, but he was able to do so because she protected him, by reassuring him.

Before they married, but after they had begun to live together, Margaret became pregnant with twins. The day she discovered she was pregnant her mother, to whom she had been very close, died. The babies eventually died, four and a half months later, stillborn. Such events can divide people, as we saw with Gwen and Howard. But the tragedies drew them closer and consolidated their commitment to each other. It drew them together, says Mark, through '. . . talking together, by being there for each other, by being able to help, to encourage. I had to give Margaret as much support as I could.' He worried for her state of mind, however, because she was the one 'whose body they came from' as he says, even though 'we both lost children.' For Margaret, it confirmed something which she already knew: 'He came home and he just took over completely.' She could depend on him. And he brought her up from the depths of despondency: 'I didn't want to talk to anybody, I didn't want to do anything. He just sort of talked me through it, you know – "It's all right, we're still young, we can have more babies." He was very good.'

And the event also confirmed for them that 'we both just wanted children.' They would go on and try to have children again. Within a short time their first son, Mark, was born. Mark senior was still in the Navy, and though he came home for the birth, he was away for the next few months of his first son's life. Leaving when this baby was just five days old was 'a gut-wrenching experience. I just didn't want to be apart from them because the baby was a part of both Margaret and myself . . . It was difficult going away. I couldn't bear to be apart from them, and of course, when I came back I'd been away for three months . . . The baby then was as much mine as Margaret's. With her having had the baby for three months, I felt it was my responsibility to take care of him just as much as she had . . . I couldn't just let her look after the baby constantly all the time . . . I felt I was the father now, not just the husband, and had to care for my child just as much as she cared for him. So I did just as much as she did – I changed the nappies, I made the bottles, I fed him at four o'clock in the morning . . . I did that with my second son, as well.'

Mark eventually left the Navy and found work as a chemical engineer. During their married life Margaret has worked, on and off, in pubs nearby. They very much wanted more children after Mark was born and tried, though with no success, until Liam was born when Mark was nine years old. But during all this time they had a full household, looking after Margaret's younger sister, nursing Mark's mother and Margaret's father, and housing many of her relatives.

Mark and Margaret had come from very different up-bringings, both with difficulties and sadness. Margaret's family is large, close-knit and fun-loving. Mark's is not so close and, as I have noted, without the same vivacity. Neither set of parents had happy marriages. Mark's father left his family when Mark was nine, leaving his mother to bring up three sons, of whom Mark was the eldest. Mark became the man of the house, helping his mother to look after his younger brothers and developing a finely-honed sense of responsibility. While not an unhappy family, humour, pleasure and enjoyment were not a big part of family life. Instead it felt like a hard life: 'My mother worked hard and did a very good job of looking after us, and we pulled together, the four of us. But I guess I decided that I was never going to do that – leave my family. I would be a different kind of husband and father.'

Margaret's father and mother stayed together, but their marriage was not terribly happy. 'It was all right as marriages go,' says Margaret. Her father went out with his mates down to the pub most nights. 'What I'd seen around, where I was brought up – Friday and Saturday night everybody went out – everybody had a good time. But it seemed to be normal for some man to be hitting his wife in the street on a Friday or Saturday night. And I thought – there's no way any man is going to hit me. Also with my parents' marriage, my dad was hardly ever there. He didn't like the responsibility of children. I'm not saying he didn't love us, because he probably did in his way, but he was always sort of wandering off somewhere, if you like. You know, he'd go missing for a few days and then come back. And I thought, "I don't want that; I don't want that either." My father never kept a job, never. And I thought, "I'm not having that either." So I knew what I was looking for.' Like Irene, like Obi, these two saw what they did not have and determined to get it, almost as if their blueprint for a happy marriage was like a photographic negative.

The biggest hurdle was Mark fitting into Margaret's large and exuberant family. But, as we have seen, he was undaunted and quickly became adept. Margaret's family not only lives nearby, at various times her sister, her brother and his family, her father, (not to mention Mark's mother) have actually lived with them. This has not felt so much a hardship as a chance to have a good time – the more the merrier. The family joke and 'take the mickey out of each other', as Margaret says, but they are not cruel. 'You know just how far you can go, and you don't push it.' Her siblings still live nearby and they have family parties every few months, usually at Margaret and Mark's house.

Margaret may have brought to the marriage her heritage of vitality, but Mark's sense of responsibility is part of what keeps this relationship steady. 'Everything has always been down the middle. Mark helps, does his part, sees if I need anything.' And as we have seen, when the children were born, child-care was split down the middle.

These days they spend a lot of their time with their boys, playing ball or board games, or watching television, but a large part of their leisure time is also spent with Margaret's relatives and their children. When Mark takes Liam to school, he also takes Margaret's niece. When he drives somewhere on an errand (Margaret does not drive) he often does additional jobs for her sister. And these days they feel they treasure 'the warmth generated' by the relationship they have and the home they have made. They love each other's company. Margaret says, 'I think we work because we actually like each other. We enjoy each other.' Their children 'just add to the enjoyment. They're part of it. They joke the way we do.'

They are not smug or complacent, though. In fact, they can imagine even better. Mark sees the advent of the children leaving home bringing them even closer together because 'we'll have more time.' And if they eventually have a little more money '. . . we can do more things together.' When you watch them throughout a typical week together you are struck by the laughter, the clear delight they take in each other, and the physicality of their relationship. They touch, they cuddle, they nuzzle and they banter. They playfully hit each other. This is a couple who do know how to have fun.

But it is also a couple who work at their relationship, maintaining a commitment to making time to share activities together, to have time on their own, to talk about anything and everything, to disclose their feelings, and thereby to keep their interest and knowledge of each other constantly updated. Without giving attention to their pleasure, committing time and energy to stoking it, this couple could become distant. Margaret could become swamped with attention to her fun-loving siblings and their families, Mark by attention to his entertaining and talented sons who play ball with him, who watch sports he likes to watch. In other words, both these people are capable of getting pleasure in many ways. It is their commitment to deriving it from each other, and their efforts to find outlets and time for it that keep pleasure alive between them.

What pleasure looks like in a relationship – what it is

Pleasure includes a number of qualities, rather than a single one, but it includes:

1. The ability to delight in the other's company.
2. To find erotic satisfaction together.
3. To share a sense of humour, and to laugh together.
4. To appreciate your partner both for what he/she is and what he/she does for you.
5. To take pleasure in doing things together (such as shared hobbies or interests or discussions).
6. To feel excited in the presence of your partner or by the prospect of being with your partner and to feel pleased or excited that he/she does so about you.
7. To get satisfaction from joint projects together, such as creating a family, or a house, or a garden, or the telling of joint stories.
8. To have delight or warm feelings about a shared history

together as well as the prospect of a shared future together.

The list of pleasurable behaviours is not reproduced for you to assess yourself and your partner against. First, ask which if any of these your partner could improve upon and then ask what you think your partner would say about *you* in terms of these behaviours over the past week, month, and year:

1. The ability to delight in the other's company.
2. To find erotic satisfaction together.
3. To share a sense of humour, and to laugh together.
4. To appreciate your partner both for what he/she is and what he/she does for you.
5. To take pleasure in doing things together (such as shared hobbies or interests or discussions).
6. To feel excited in the presence of your partner or by the prospect of being with your partner and to feel pleased or excited that he/she does so about you.
7. To get satisfaction from joint projects together, such as creating a family, or a house, or a garden, or the telling of joint stories.
8. To have delight or warm feelings about a shared history together, as well as the prospect of a shared future together.

PART TWO

How Couples Can Stay On Course and Maintain Protective Love

CHAPTER NINE

Maintaining Love Despite Obstacles: Upward and Downward Spirals

Why did Irene and John survive years rent by ugliness? Irene's irritability and intolerance could well have destroyed them. If John had responded with disappointment in her, nursing his pain and building it into resentment, and if Irene had not expressed gratitude, thereby stopping her contribution to the downward spiral, this couple might not have survived. It took a conscious effort, a struggle to override, (in John's case) the impulsive, self-protective, first response to an aggressive remark or action on Irene's part. After all, aggression breeds defensiveness and ultimately can breed more aggression. It took a different reading of Irene's behaviour by John, so that he looked beyond the aggressive content and found a suffering woman. That act bred Irene's gratitude, which healed them in the end. For John, while this was difficult because it required patience and tolerance, it became habitual, especially as Irene eventually rewarded him with her return to 'the old Irene'. To override a first response to an aggressive, rejecting or disrespectful parry is very difficult. But it is what is required in intimate relationships. People often confuse intimacy with throwing out the rules of courtesy, permitting impulsive acts. In the case of moments of conflict or emotional distress, intimacy lived this way can become dangerous.

Even in marriages which began with the five factors (which is probably most, at the beginning), obstacles lie in wait. Obstacles which sometimes block love permanently. Many, maybe even most, well-intentioned couples go off the course of lasting love, into downward spirals.

Couples are initially thrown off by normally occurring obstacles. These are 'transition points', such as the birth of children, which shake up a couple's habitual routines and expectations. In their wake inevitably come stress and distress, and sometimes they develop into crises. Couples also frequently (although not inevitably) encounter additional obstacles, the abnormal crises of life, or its unexpected traumas and misfortunes such as grave illness, untimely death of loved ones, or job loss. Each transition, whether normal or abnormal, poses a dilemma for the couple around the issues of protection, focus, gratitude and balance.

What I mean by a *dilemma* is this: each couple has a choice. Partners can either summon energy or not – energy being in critically short supply during hard times – to provide the necessary protective caring for the partner's welfare, also at this time giving particular attention or focus, and also showing particular gratitude. To draw the energy this requires at such times is counter-instinctive, which is why it is difficult. When under siege, instincts lead people to protect themselves and their young first. But the preservation of the partner has to be felt to be *as important* as the preservation of the self. His or her protection must be felt *as if* you are protecting your young. This is what John was doing when he did not react to the aggressive Irene, but saw the suffering one behind her. As this is counter-instinctive, it is these difficult times, when you are indeed under siege, in need yourself of care, focus,

146

and protection, which are most testing of relationships. Consequently, these times become dilemmas precisely because couples *do* have the choice to do the hard thing (the counter-instinctive one) or not. It must become a conscious choice.

This consciousness about setting things right between you is what many researchers and writers on love have meant by the 'hard work' of relationships[1]. There is probably no respectable research on the maintenance of love which does not in some way point to the need for a degree of self-consciousness about changing your own behaviour: putting yourself in the other's shoes; being 'heroic' by biting your tongue or admitting your faults or apologising; or rejigging your timetable, commitments and priorities to devote increasingly scarce time, attention and energy to your partner.

All of this is hard work and flies in the face of romantic notions about love. 'But I'm not an expressive person!' people in marital therapy tell me when I suggest that they need to tell their partner explicitly when they have appreciated something. You can see the groan inside written on their faces, as if they are feeling stuck gears being pushed to change. 'Say thank you – for putting the rubbish out?' You can see them trying to imply that I must be crazy, although they know it is not a crazy suggestion, it's just the effort, the pushing aside habits of years, required for this huge, even momentous shift.

The theory of protective love proposes a way forward for couples by making this choice conscious. The further a couple goes off-course, into a deep downward spiral of anger, resentment and alienation, the harder it is to summon the energy to reverse the process, to make the partner someone needing care and protection. Failure to do so breeds unloving, unprotective behaviour on both sides. It is a very perilous dynamic. Persistent failure to love, blocked in this way by these obstacles, can become permanent.

The upward and downward spirals: staying in love v. falling out of it

A couple's poor resolution of a transition or crisis can mean they can enter a *downward spiral* of resentment and anger. But equally, if they manage the transition, they can enter an *upward spiral* of reinforced and reinforcing loving. Most couples want to stay on course, and indeed, in the early years manage it. Most marriages begin happily. Thereafter come tests, the repeated transitions or crises. In the face of the ensuing difficulty members of a couple may fail to receive or deliver the protection, or focus, or gratitude needed to sustain each other through it. They enter a downward spiral where they slowly lose focus on each other, consistently need but consistently fail to get protection; then, instead of feeling gratitude, they gradually become resentful and frustrated. The downward spiral is marked by withdrawal, lack of loyalty, de-focusing on the other's needs and interests, resentment, frustration, and perhaps envy.

To get into an upward spiral, and, more fundamentally, to stay there, requires the first, essential step: couples who are happy accept the need for protection and the centrality of their relationship in their lives. They give each other necessary focus. They express or demonstrate gratitude. They reciprocate protection, focus and gratitude. The unusual few, who remain in love, steer the course, strengthening their unions through transitions or crises. The essential ingredients operate, breeding further strength and love. Couples who will never sustain happiness deny the need for protection, and refuse to accept that this is also true of their partners.

As we saw in Chapter 3, Jackie and Obi had an enormous row over moving house, which frightened them deeply; they clashed because what would make one feel secure risked the security of the other. This row, which resulted in Jackie leaving temporarily, threatened to tip the couple into a downward spiral. But smaller domestic conflicts over the years together had given them a successful strategy and perspective to over-come this larger disruption to their lives. As Jackie described earlier, her equilibrium was severely tested by their neighbour; eventually she suffered migraines, and was particularly worried when she became pregnant. The problem was that Obi did not think that moving was practical. He argued that interest rates were at an all-time high, and he had only begun to climb the ladder at his accountancy firm. Moving at that point would put them in a precarious position. Financial security is a pivotal part of Obi's sense of security. He worries about money, he tries to save it, and having enough in reserve is particularly comforting to him. Who could win in this conflict, for if one won, the other's sense of security would be under attack? In fact, the row became a battle, with Jackie leaving in a rage. What each did next is what made the difference between entering a downward and an upward spiral.

Jackie spent the night first calming down, and then trying to 'put myself in his shoes'. She tried to 'think like Obi'. In doing this, she saw that in the long run, if she just waited a bit longer the interest rates would go down, or they would have saved up a bit more money, and eventually they would move. She still wanted to move, but she could live with staying for the moment. She returned in this frame of mind.

Obi spent the night in a similar fashion. 'If she wants it that much, then it will work out somehow,' he thought. When they got together again, both now calmer and both having not only understood but felt the other's position (putting themselves in the other's 'shoes'), they returned to partner-ship, to a generosity to the other. The interest rates went down almost immediately, in any case, and they did end up moving. But the generosity of spirit which yielded each one's ability to feel for the other is what produced the upward spiral they then entered. Buying their house together was a large step, as they said, in 'sealing our partnership'. The upward spiral began; focus increased as they talked through the move, and made plans for the house; gratitude grew as they both acknowledged the other's generosity in coming to understand the opposing position; balance was fostered through the joint enterprise of house-buying, with plans for decorating, furnishing and pulling it all together. Pleasure grew as they shared this new, exciting enterprise.

Would you say you are in an upward or downward spiral at the moment? To try to see what might be associated with these spirals, this **exercise** is designed to get you to be sensitive to potential stressors for both you and your partner, in the form of external events or conditions, in your relationship. Try to see what else was going on for you and your partner during both the upward and downward spirals. (You may need your diary for this.)

1. If you are currently in an upward spiral, make a list of at least three external things going on at the time for you and then do the same for your partner.
2. Then think of the last difficult period you have had together. Do the same as in number 1 above. These are among stressors you both have to look out for in the future and also be sensitive to; they have and probably will again incite a neediness and vulnerability in your and in your partner.

If you are in a downward spiral, do number 1 and 2 above in reverse.

CHAPTER TEN

Unavoidable Obstacles: Transition Points

Anyone who has been in a long-term marriage, or who has lived through what psychologists of family life call 'transition points in the family life cycle' knows that, day-to-day, marital life is difficult. Silvery moonlight, wine and roses – the stuff of romance and passion – are really beside the point. What we all want and need is a refuge and protection from the assault of daily upheavals, and married people look for it from each other. Moreover, certain periods bring daily tests of protection and focus, particularly when there are children. In the normal course of events, in marriage we both expect and feel gratitude for help and understanding in managing these upheavals. But also in the normal course of events we become angry, resentful and frustrated if that help is not forthcoming. The upward and downward spirals are inbuilt in the normal course of things.

Points of transition in marriage are points of stress, difficulty and differences within couples[1]. They are normal and expectable; necessarily they are times of stress. Transition points can be a couple's breaking point, or the source of it. They test couples' reserves of support, the quality of their

151

mutual focus and their energy to give the time or support each member may need. It is after a transition point or in the midst of one that most marriages break down. They are periods in which couples can either deepen love, through appreciation of each other's efforts, or diminish it, through anger, resentment and frustration. They are times in which couples can enter an *upward*, or *downward spiral*.

These marital transitions include the stress and conflict of loyalties inherent in forming a marital unit (the beginning); the upheavals consequent to the birth of children (the early years); the sometimes more gradual but nevertheless disruptive 'letting go' phase, as children grow up and leave (the middle years); and the tensions attendant to the resumption of life alone together, years which include in their span diminishment of time and energy on career, and often retirement and illness (the later years)[2]. Some types of crises or transitions lend themselves less easily to the making and instead more easily to the breaking of relationships. These are ones in which both partners need high degrees of protection, focus and gratitude at the same time. It is hard to be a 'protector' regarding your spouse's needs and feelings, asking, 'What does he/she need now? How can I help?' if you feel under siege yourself. In contrast, a crisis in which one person is clearly more upset and affected than another is probably a kind which binds couples closer together more easily. In such cases it is more clear-cut that one needs more looking after than the other.

Divided loyalties: forming a marital unit (the beginning)

Many couples find it difficult to make the transition of first loyalty from birth families to their marital or cohabitation partnerships. This is partly because, no matter how committed, the early years of these adult relationships cannot compare to most parent-child relationships, for loyalty and safety – nor for protection and focus, in particular. It is also because parents usually have an even more difficult time entrusting their children's safety and loyalty to new partners; to free their children enough to devote first loyalty to their partners may be impossible for some. This tension then gets played out in the difficult choices demanded between the two sides.

For example, six months after their marriage, and three years after they had met, Jean left Stuart for two months to look after her ill mother, at her father's request. Though Stuart made only the mildest protest at the time, this separation proved very damaging to the couple. Stuart made a few noises about Jean's brothers helping out instead of her. She responded furiously, accusing Stuart of asking her to abandon her parents at the hour of their greatest need; in any case, she had no moral choice but to go. Stuart acquiesced. It was only in retrospect that both acknowledged the decision for Jean to go had been a bad one for the couple.

They had recently moved to a new city many hundreds of miles away from Jean's parents. Stuart knew only one other couple there and, being shy, he made few efforts to get together with them. In their frequent telephone conversations, Jean was preoccupied with details of settling her mother into appropriate treatment. Stuart seemed to listen sympathetically, but on Jean's return he was sullen, withdrawn and wholly focused on his antipathy for his new job. This disaffection predominated over every aspect of their life; Stuart saw no point in making new friends or exploring the city as he had decided that moving out of it was the only solution. He was irritable around Jean, and their sex life was non-existent. The decline of their relationship became fixed on the growing list of small and large irritations between them, from Jean's sloppy housekeeping to Stuart's boredom with anything in which she showed interest.

Years later, Jean looked back on that terrible time and said, 'I made a mistake, abandoning him. My parents shouldn't have asked me to do that, leave my husband for two months when he had no other support but me. But then I always had dropped everything for them before, so why should they have thought otherwise?'

Having children (the early years)

The first years of having children have been documented as the most stressful for marriage[3]. Even divorce statistics reflect this: most marriages break up after around nine years, or, in other words, after the slow attenuation of the marital bond under the strain of the early child-rearing years.

Even starting with pregnancy, parenthood seems to have its divisive elements. Psychoanalytic literature records the, theoretically, difficult adjustment men have to make to their wives carrying another being. This is a possibly ripe time for men to have affairs as already they are feeling displaced. Women have themselves written about their own bodily and emotional preoccupation during pregnancy, which unites them with other women but disunites them from men.

Certain transition points are testing precisely because they shake up each spouse almost equally. One such transition point is the birth of a baby. At first, the new mother may seem more needy and overwhelmed, especially if she has undergone a difficult birth, and especially if she is the primary carer. The adjustment and disruptions in her life will be consequently more insistent, direct and profound than those in the new father's. But, having said that, there are of course deep repercussions on the husbands' lives as well. It is a transition which often begins the process of division between husband and wife, intensified by this differential of mutual strain. A new father, overwhelmed himself, may be numb to his wife's need for help, tenderness and support, and crushed by the new dependence on him. In many cases, the plummeting marital satisfaction which begins at this point stays down all the way through the child-rearing years.

'In the beginning,' recounts Iona, 'Joe wasn't around so much . . . when I had David (their first child) he was jealous. And although he loves David . . . he's blown his stack, he's really lost his temper and he's said horrible things . . . I did resent Joe a bit, because I felt that if ever David was naughty like children are, instead of Joe being a little bit liberal with him, he was heavy with him, which hurt me to the quick. And of course those were times when we argued. Lots of couples do row over the children. . . . Joe was working very hard to try to make a home for us, really. But the thing was, he did miss out on David's upbringing because he was working all the hours he could, and when he got home in the evening David was normally in bed, so he only really saw him at weekends. And, of course, I had David all the time so we were very close, and then when Joe did get some time off he obviously saw how close we were and it frightened him.'

Frequency and satisfaction with sex declines sharply in the early years of having children (especially of course just post-childbirth), with the concomitant decline of intimacy within the couple. This is also a time in which couples (particularly men) are susceptible to affairs in part because of this. Men have been reported to feel pushed aside to the margins of family life[4]. While they may develop close relationships with their children, these are usually less close than those between mother and children, and with fewer opportunities for the couple to have time together on their own, the husband may have a more distant emotional relationship with his wife as well. This distance breeds dissatisfaction, posing a strain on what may have been a close relationship before children.

Linda and Tom married when they were post-graduate students at the same university. They met through mutual friends, had wonderful sex and tremendous fun together and married two years later. They shared a lot of activities – they sailed, walked, swam together twice a week, played tennis together daily when the weather permitted and loved to have and go to parties. After four years Linda gave birth to their first child. Tom had received a large grant, in his first job as a lecturer. He had a lab and graduate students of his own and was determined to make a name for himself in his field. Linda had taken a much lower-profile career path, opting to do part-time research in preparation for having a family. During their first two years as parents, Linda, through choice, took primary responsibility for their baby: took him to the doctor, took off work when he was ill, arranged childcare, planned outings with other mothers and children and looked after the house. Tom would be home on fewer and fewer evenings. Soon it became his practice to work at his lab at weekends as well. Soon there was only one reliable part of the week reserved for each other – Sunday afternoon – and these often included other people, family who visited on Sundays, and always included the baby.

The erosion of their relationship was gradual and out of their consciousness, until Linda began to unburden herself to their GP. At the GP's suggestion that Linda seemed depressed, but more tellingly that he was alarmed for their marriage, Linda was stunned into action, which included a demand to get professional help before it was too late. Twelve years later (and another son), this couple are once again sharing time, activities and pleasure, sometimes with their two sons, and sometimes now on their own.

Children growing up and beginning to leave (the middle years)

The middle years of parenthood, which often coincide with approaching or advancing middle age, put different strains upon a marriage. This transition involves the following:

1. Children becoming more independent, leaving parents more time in which they may or may not choose to spend

more together, on the one hand, and also making demands on parents to pull together over questions of how much choice and independence they want to give these older children. This is a particular strain, as it tests the sharing of values. If the couple has become emotionally estranged this testing can have an even more divisive effect; moreover, if they do not move into the vacuum left by their children's independence towards increased time and focus on each other, they are making a statement about the relatively low priority each has for the other. Such a statement, even if implicit and unremarked on, does not go emotionally unnoticed.

Sally and Paul have three daughters. One is disabled and, unable to care for her, the couple have recently found for her a residential placement. Their other two daughters have also recently left home, one to do a year abroad before university and the other, the oldest, to do a post-graduate course, also abroad. Sally works as an administrative assistant part-time, but her real passion is gardening. Paul runs his own business in the small city in which they live.

Sally looks older than her 54 years as she sighs and admits with deflation: 'I've stopped wishing and hoping that things would change. In the beginning, when we just had the one at home I thought, "Right, next year we can travel. Next year we can just take off for the weekend, and go exploring." Or, because Paul runs his own business I'd think, "He can control his hours and if there's a garden show on he could come with me! We could develop the garden together; he always said he wanted to learn how to do it as well as I can!" But he's not interested. He never has time. This isn't what I'd looked forward to. My widowed and divorced friends all know how to be alone. I sometimes wonder if it's worth staying married. I could be alone and be having fun with them instead. Maybe that's what I should do. I didn't get married just to have kids, but it looks like that's what I did.'

2. Career: as people enter middle age they are consolidating their work lives, as fewer choices will remain in the future as they age. It is a time for reflection about the direction of your work life, what you have and what you want to have achieved. For those who have never seriously entered the work market, or who have taken time away from it, the same considerations apply with a 'now-or-never' sense to them if returning to work is an option.

3. A general life review, including relationships, emotional state, physical appearance and health occurs. People start to think in terms of years left to live, rather than a vague, unending stretch of time ahead of them[5]. A recent study by Terri Apter of women in their early and middle middle-age also notes that at least some (and, indeed, most) of these women looked ahead towards the second part of their lives with a sense of optimism and confidence, but always with the knowledge that they were looking into a shrinking (if better) time span. Within this perspective, people tend to find themselves critiquing their relationships, or feeling vaguely discontented, disillusioned, or consumed by preoccupations about what they have not yet experienced or achieved. In this perspective, things often feel more intolerable than they had before (or would after). Coupled with increasing freedom and time, since children are older, this dissatisfaction can lead people into affairs[6], particularly if someone appears with just those qualities the partner lacks.

Joanna is a librarian, married for 21 years to Peter, a mathematical engineer. They have a comfortable relationship, but one in which passion died long ago, and in which Joanna felt she could not 'talk to Peter the way I could with my real friends. His eyes glaze over when I talk. He's lost in the clouds. Doing equations or something. He's just not interested in the things I am. But he is a very good man. A nice man. I love him in my way, but I don't feel close to him, and now I can't have sex with him. It was never really right and I just know I couldn't have talked to him about it. He's just not like that. It would have embarrassed him far too much.' But Joanna fantasised about other men, and finally one day a man she had known slightly, who used her section of the library frequently, who had flirted mildly with her over the years, asked her out for a coffee. They talked for two hours, non-stop and 'I was completely, utterly in love by the second cup of coffee.' Joanna and this man have had an on-again, off-again affair for five years. 'The sex is terrific, we understand each other completely. But I cannot leave Peter, at least not yet. I just can't make the move; it would destroy him, and then how could I be happy, how could I live with myself?'

The post-children couple (the later years)

For a couple in this stage of the marital life cycle, the transition to being a couple without children, if they have had them, means a fundamental change. If there has been a gradual emotional estrangement over the child-rearing years, living together alone can intensify frustration and resentment. On the other hand, without the divisiveness which children can sometimes engender, such couples can find their way back towards each other.

For any couple there are decisions, often out of conscious-ness, about how much time, and time doing what, they should now expend together. Demands on them as grandparents, or from outside interests (hobbies, gardening, other friend-ships) for which there is also now time, force decisions about priorities upon them. Again, choices which preclude focusing on each other send powerful emotional messages, while choices made in favour of it can knit them together more intimately. This can be a time of particular strain when one member of a couple has been expecting that more of the time will now be spent together and the other does not.

For example, Pat and Barry were a couple in their fifties, whose last child had just left for university, when Barry was suddenly made redundant from his executive-level job. After two years of job-seeking, they reluctantly concluded that, apart from the occasional consulting job, Barry was now formally retired. The result of these events was to render Barry deeply depressed and Pat to speak of divorce. Barry was a fish out of water with his new-found 'freedom', and in reaction Pat was beside herself with rage. 'Why can't he take pleasure in all this extra time? Why can't he come up with ideas? He could join me gardening. He could take language classes with me. We could travel. We could move to a smaller, more manageable place which would free up money so we could spend it on doing things for ourselves.' Clearly she had been contemplating their retirement years in advance, imagining the fun together which she had put on hold while raising their children. When asked how he had imagined their later years Barry drew a blank. 'I never thought about it,' he said, as if it were still a novel thought. 'I only saw myself working. That's all.'

The resentment that Pat felt was palpable. Barry had failed to read her mind, to know her wishes. He kept on failing, and Pat's anger kept mounting. The failure of years of avoiding focusing on each other, years of letting pleasure between them die, years of expecting to be understood, valued and looked after and being disappointed erupted into a flood of anger and resentment. The downward spiral was so profound that this couple could not recover.

But Joe and Iona form a contrast: the birth of David, their first son, could have sent them into a downward spiral, but did not. As we have seen, Iona admits that the birth of their first son posed a problem in her relationship with Joe. He felt pushed out, jealous of the boy, punishing him more severely than Iona felt was merited. Her sympathy and understanding of how Joe felt helped to curb her initial hurt response, so that it did not grow into resentment. Instead, she felt protective and redoubled her efforts to show Joe how much she loved him through her usual means, such as cooking for him, buying him special things, being affectionate with him, listening to him and sharing her stories and insights with him. She wished that Joe had become more involved with David than he did, or as much as he did become with Ian, but, protectively and appreciatively, she came to the notion that Joe was performing his role as father in the way he knew best at the time, by working hard and earning a good living. She did not harangue him for not being home. This helped to make Joe feel appreciated – and protected – and he was able to continue to be loving in kind to her. What could have escalated into a drifting apart through resentment was curbed through the enactment of the five factors.

Abnormal crises

Abnormal crises or obstacles include illness at an early age, disability, untimely death (such as of children), and other unexpected losses (such as of job, or home). Each of these crises pose obstacles to the easy provision of protection, focus, pleasure, gratitude and balance. Each of the essential factors are tested in these times.

When Tina and Andrew's fourteen-year-old daughter was admitted to hospital with a severe eating disorder they both felt as if their world had collapsed. Over the next two years their daughter was in and out of hospitals. When she was at home her symptoms were particularly testing for the family, with her rituals around food making family meal times almost impossible, and with attempts to get her to eat exhausting and mostly unsuccessful.

Most of this burden fell on Tina. Andrew left for work early in the morning, and often came home late at night. This pattern became exaggerated over the period of their daughter's severe illness. Instead of truncating his work responsibilities, Andrew seemed to be increasing them, volunteering for jobs which demanded more time from him. In addition, when he was home, when the rituals would start, Andrew would cover his ears. More than once he left the house. When Tina, broken and exhausted, sobbed and cried for help, he responded with, 'Well, what do you want me to do? I've tried everything. You've tried everything. I can't make her eat.' When their younger son became alarmingly ill with flu and suspected meningitis and Andrew's response to Tina's desperate phone call to him at work was to ask her to phone him later with any news, she decided to leave him. A few months later she initiated divorce proceedings.

John and Nina's story, told earlier, of the loss of their first baby, illustrates how the enactment of protectiveness, balance, focus and gratitude enabled this couple to pull together and be strengthened by the crisis. In the first instance, John saw that, despite his own terror and pain, he had to protect Nina first and foremost, as she was the one who had lost the baby, the one who had been through the gruelling and ultimately unproductive labour. The wish to protect her was so strong it pushed aside his own grief for a time. Eventually Nina herself, when she had recovered physically, was keen to talk to John about his own sense of grief. 'We talked and talked,' they both say. And shed tears and told each other things, as John said, things which he had been holding back, and in that time John knew that he could trust Nina completely. He felt completely secure and protected with her.

Also during that time, this couple learned that the other had admirable qualities – and each expressed their appreciation to the other. 'John could talk to all the doctors, get the whole picture. He could take charge. The "big shoulders" which my mother felt my father had – he had them, I learned,' says Nina, while John learned that 'Nina could be strong and independent. She could be tough and get through things.' Each feels grateful to the other for those respective qualities.

Instead of licking their wounds separately, they tried to

understand what each was feeling; 'I learned about Nina, and I know I let that last little bit I might have been holding out go then,' says John. The talking and listening and feeling understood are part of what is necessary for most people to overcome grief. This couple could use each other for support in the most intimate way, and learned about each other through such time, attention and honesty. Each had his or her turn. The balance was struck and helped to create the trust each developed in the other.

The crucial elements in the responses of this couple illustrate the importance of the six factors:

1. There was an awareness on both sides of the gift each was making. Both spouses were conscious that what their partner was doing required awareness of the other's need and a choice to sacrifice something to help the other.

2. Each was able to receive the gift from the other. The old saying 'giving is better than receiving' is, like all sayings, a wise one even in the deconstruction of love. It is apposite here in part, because of the pleasure given to the spouse who gave time and energy being able to do so and being recognised for the gift.

3. This couple felt, acknowledged and expressed in some way gratitude for the gift each had given in a time of need.

4. The balance of this function of love, which we can see most clearly when couples are managing crises, is also a crucial element. Protection given – if recognised, received and acknowledged – usually breeds protection given. Thereby, first gratitude and then love are fostered.

5. What preceded all of these was the knowledge that the

163

person in the shared 'crisis' was vulnerable, in need of an alliance which offered protection or support or help.

6. And, crucially, this couple experienced pleasure in the transition they shared. Their pleasure together was increased. They have banked another shared experience which brings pleasure in the memory and increased pleasure in the living through the transition itself.

CHAPTER ELEVEN

The Mechanisms for Understanding Each Other: Increasing Protection

Valerie and James kept getting into the same argument: she could not trust him. He kept in extensive communication with his ex-wife in an attempt to placate her, lest she turn their children against him. This made Valerie desperately insecure: she felt James's ex-wife still had designs on him. She also knew that the ex-wife was manipulative enough to try to ensnare James, whom she cast as naive, without his being aware of it. The argument was always sparked by Valerie's discovery of some contact between the ex-spouses. They then spun out of control, with recriminations on both sides. On Valerie's, they were that James was weak, without insight and disrespectful of her feelings. On James's, they were that Valerie was mistrustful, needlessly jealous and selfishly unfeeling towards his emotional predicament regarding his children. They spiralled into such acrimonious character assassinations that relations remained soured between them for days. During this time many other trivial behaviours between them would be screened through their respectively unforgiving lenses, and distortions and mis-attributions would result. James, for example, would find Valerie's clothes all over the bedroom, and catalogue it as another example of her selfish, uncaring attitude towards him. Valerie would register that James had not given her a phone message from her mother; she would read that as James being disrespectful. The building blocks of many more grudges and resentments were in place; in time, these would almost certainly grow into walls of resentment and contempt. In such ways many lovers lose their love.

This couple sought marital therapy before the wall had been permanently erected, while there was enough motivation, will and ability to believe in the other's good to put energy into correcting their behaviours and growing mis-perceptions of each other. An outline of what they did in therapy can serve to show how couples can reverse this pernicious process of the breakdown of love.

The programme of therapy which is outlined, which stresses the use of particular techniques and strategies, has been developed in my marital therapy work over twenty years, as well as with supervisees and students, work which has dealt with hundreds of couples, and is guided in large part by which is known as an 'integrative problem-centred approach'[1]. This stresses both achieving an insight into the source of the problem, and also working in the most parsimonious way to change the destructive patterns within a couple which have become habitual and which themselves have become the problem. The focus is on trying to educate people to new ways of behaving with each other, teaching them how to negotiate their needs and desires from each other, but only being able to do so when they are able to understand what has been blocking them from behaving in better ways towards each other. In the work I describe, which is in this way a variant of the problem-centred approaches written about before, the insight which has the potential to unblock people is that into their respective vulnerability and the need for a partner's protection. The techniques for trying to change behaviour follow the acquisition of this insight, which will usually melt resentment and anger and begin the process of opening the couple up to different solutions to the problem of how to behave more lovingly and constructively towards each other.

Gaining insight into each partner's vulnerability, to create protectiveness

First, the work with James and Valerie was focused on gaining insight, and as we know, in particular, insight into their respective vulnerability. It was described, then validated, by each through a vivid recounting of their own experience, in the particular ways each partner was essentially vulnerable, looking for a primary protective alliance with the other, rather than a vengeful, selfish one, interested in exploiting the partner. The way this point most applied in Valerie and James's case is that Valerie felt insecure, afraid that James's loyalty and past ties to his first family, and especially to his children, would predominate over his loyalty to her, and she would lose him. The prospect of this was terrible to her; she would be bereft without him. James, for his part, felt as deep a tie to his children as he did to Valerie, but was afraid that Valerie wanted him to give up his children in favour of her; he feared that her insecurity was such that she was jealous of his love for them and that he would be forced to make a terrible choice. He was also afraid that his children would reject him if his former wife manipulated them into doing so, and so he tried to placate her. This left Valerie more vulnerable. But harping on her insecurity rendered James even more afraid that she would wreck his relationship with his children.

These were not difficult insights to achieve, but they were pieces of knowledge overlooked by each partner in the accumulation of defensiveness and recriminations between themselves. Both wanted support. Understanding just how vulnerable each felt was key to reversing the build-up of damage.

There are some strategies to achieve this insight which may be useful to try:

a. Achieving empathy

To reach insight takes a degree of *empathy*, and to achieve this means laying psychological armour and defensiveness aside. This is both difficult and essential to do. Empathy takes imagination – you must feel as if you are the other person; you must imagine yourself into a situation in which you have felt exactly that kind of vulnerability yourself.

An **exercise** used in acting, in which you imagine yourself a fictitious third person, is a way in to achieving this. For example, to understand how another feels vulnerable, afraid of loss and of being left alone, bereft, you can imagine yourself as a small child. Your mother announces she is leaving. You have no power to make her stay. You feel as if you have a hole in your heart, yet you cannot tell her because you cannot find the words, and you are afraid to make her too angry or too sad to want to see you again. You cannot understand why this terrible thing is happening. You feel terrified and powerless all at once, so you start to scream and throw your favourite doll on to the pavement, where it breaks. You don't know why. Your mother gets angry, and you lose her gentle support, the one thing you most need. You feel worse; you feel bereft and as vulnerable, lost and powerless as possible.

A more concrete and direct approach is usually possible. Most people can remember quite easily just how it feels to be so nakedly vulnerable. Putting yourself back, imaginatively, into a remembered painful, or insecure, or damaged state (which may feel risky; you need to remind yourself explicitly as you do this that 'I am only imagining; this is history') can achieve the effect more directly and dramatically. In this imaginatively remembered state you can then connect with your partner's feelings of insecurity, of terror of losing someone you love, of being rejected with no recourse. In times of conflict, the threat of being out of partnership can feel like an echo of that. That is probably how your partner feels. Connecting this way with your own experiences in your own past, whether as a small child or as a grown-up, both achieves the requisite empathy and also simultaneously increases a sense of partnership and intimacy.

Sometimes it is possible to reach people's imagination through appealing to how it would feel to their own children to be put in such situations – most parents have some direct access to how children (especially small children) feel un-protected. The point in such empathy is that each person must then, in the present, experience an emotional connection with the painful emotion the partner describes. To do so is not to admit responsibility for provoking those feelings (even if you may have done). It is simply to listen to them clearly, not to negate them, and to acknowledge their validity even if they do not fit the present facts. Once they have got the point about vulnerability and the need for a protective alliance, and felt it through the exercise of empathy, couples can benefit from a well-established strategy for maintaining their insight. This strategy is called 'reframing'.

b. Reframing

Reframing is a technique used primarily in family systems therapy, often to great effect[2]. It entails putting a positive connotation on things which previously have been given a negative connotation. It is a technique which puts a benign perspective on your partner's behaviour and feelings (actually 'framing' it differently). Instead of viewing your partner's actions as if they are against you or without concern for you, you frame his actions as those of a person on some emotional precipice, with the unintentional fall-out that you are hurt or disregarded.

For example, Valerie had framed James's failure to leave her mother's telephone message for her as 'disrespectful'. Since her picture of James was that he was selfish and disrespectful, this interpretation fit into it easily. When Valerie began to perceive that James was frightened of losing her and feared his children would reject him, her whole picture of him changed: he was, instead, a fallible, vulnerable man. Within that picture, or frame, she viewed his actions differently. When he next forgot a phone message, as he was wont to do, she saw it as disorganisation. Since before they had lived together, James had not been in the habit of writing things down; Valerie was offered a different picture in which to frame this behaviour. In this new picture Valerie *reframed* it as lack of training and habit. She bought a stack of message pads and a holder for pens, which she filled, and put these by the phone. James found this generous and enabling.

Changing the frame gives a picture which is usually not only easier to live with, but also more accurate.

But insight is only the first, if necessary step. Valerie and James had enough access to their own pain to imagine how the other must be feeling. Once tentatively acknowledged and validated, it was possible to go on. The next step was to work on the bad behaviours, which had become habitual, which provoked feelings of vulnerability, isolation, and lack of support. For this couple it was both the nature of James's contact with his former wife and Valerie's response to it. This triggered a chain of negative events. But characteristically the couple did not realise this. By the time they registered resentment, their emotional state and perceptions had become pervasive and generalised: 'He's so uncaring and dis-respectful'/'She's so selfish'. So many small events had been tagged with these labels that it was almost impossible to say why or how these feelings had come to reside between them.

However, it was important to trace them back to their

source, and so the couple kept a diary of when things began to go 'off' between them, and then what each did to maintain this 'off' state. This is called *'tracking'*.

Behavioural change

Step 1: Tracking behaviours and feelings to the source of the vulnerability

Tracking – charting feelings or behaviours back to their source through painstaking detail of what happened as a result of what, by whom and when – is a technique much used by therapists who work in various 'problem-centred' therapies. You see where you went off-course, and come up with suggestions of how you could have handled things differently, should they arise again. The idea is also that there is a pattern; the issue will arise again and the couple, now with greater awareness and a repertoire of alternative behaviours they have nominated to employ when they meet the issue again, can create a new and different path for themselves.

An exercise for tracking
Often the use of diaries by both people, who then compare the data to come up with the pathway back to the source problem is very helpful. Tracking is an essential step in correcting misattributions and distortions which then lead to behaviours which provoke further difficulties. It is a step towards then correcting these.

Valerie and James tracked their difficulties back to the arguments about James's ex-wife. The next time James made contact, he did so differently. He labelled his actions explicitly so there were fewer opportunities for misconceptions and misattributions and he acknowledged Valerie's vulnerability. He said to Valerie, 'I have to arrange a contact visit with the kids, and I'll have to speak to Kim. I'm going to be as polite as I can, but I won't talk in any depth to her. I don't want to upset you, but I also don't want to antagonise her unduly, because you know she might take it out on me through the kids. Is that all right?'

Valerie's reply was in kind. 'I know you're afraid of that. What if you limit your talk with her by telling her that you have an appointment you'll be late for, if she starts going on too long? Or tell her that I'm expecting a phone call? In other words, can we agree that you'll limit your conversation to arrangements and polite how-are-you's and to only a few minutes? If you'd agree to that beforehand, I wouldn't stand around tensely waiting for you to get off the phone, and making you feel threatened.'

Step 2: Being unspontaneous

James and Valerie became *proactive* in their behaviour to each other. Being so is artificial and awkward but absolutely necessary. Their interactions were stilted at first. Each complained that talking to the other in this way was unnatural. But talking to each other 'naturally' had produced horrendous results; had they not changed to *un*natural, they would have stayed stuck in habits of damaging behaviours and distorting assumptions.

To change habits needs premeditation and self-consciousness. In this way, change in relationships is, as we have always been warned, hard work. There is not a single researcher on love who has not in some way discovered the necessity for making the interactions between the couple conscious and consequently at times self-conscious. This is the phase we referred to in Chapter 9 as the 'dilemma': you do the counter-instinctive thing, which is not to protect yourself but your partner. You make this a conscious act. The result of this choice is that you are much more likely to receive the protective love you seek, than if you instinctively defend yourself. You resolve the dilemma by acting in an unspontaneous, premeditated, well-chosen way.

Valerie and James initially resisted my suggestions to be

unspontaneous but, desperate to change, they put them into (awkward) practice. Over time their new responses became their habits.

Valerie and James indicated in their respective responses that:

1. they had taken in the *insight* regarding their respective vulnerability and expectation for a supportive, protective alliance with their partner because of that.
2. they corrected the misattribution of the other's behaviour as 'selfish' or 'uncaring', etc. and *reframed* it as vulnerable and needy.
3. they had begun to focus on the other as much as on him- or herself.
4. they demonstrated some balance – 'I understand your point, and I will go some way towards you' and vice versa.
5. in acknowledging their own and their partner's need for protection they are demonstrating the first step in the protective loving process.

In this proactive phase, *enactment* is the key: that is, words are not enough. Actions and words are essential. As marriage is largely about negotiating delicately, these words and actions must be carefully chosen.

There are some strategies every couple can try employing to help them change their behaviours towards each other, and to negotiate sensitively. They emphasise managing your own frustration and defensiveness, taking responsibility to be as clear as possible about your intentions and responses, and planning your goal in advance, thus creating safe and trustworthy behaviour towards each other.

a. Establishing ground rules:
The couple who says, 'We never go to bed angry. If we have a disagreement we stay up until we settle it,' is a cliché. But, as with all clichés, there is a gallon of truth in it. While as a

particular strategy it is not universally applicable (for some it simply prolongs agony by institutionalising sleepless nights and strung-out days in which new disagreements mount up, further depleting scarce remaining energy), the point of the cliché is that this couple has ground rules. Sticking to them works.

Ground rules about what is acceptable and what not between couples works as a social contract does. Breaking the social contract means all hell can break loose, with crime rampant and brother cheating brother. Breaking couples' ground rules can mean the same to the couple. Ground rules establish basic boundaries of respect, based on rules of courtesy, which is fundamental to trust and love.

Couples' ground rules should include at least the following basic ones:

1. No character assassinations: 'You are a pig'/'You always do that'/'You make me feel I am lower than low'/'You never lift a finger'. Anger is a distorting emotion and conclusions about someone's character drawn in the heat of it are usually wrong. This is especially true for your lover. Only a moment before you may have felt love for him or her. Suddenly it feels as if you were all wrong, this person is really a cad. Anger inflates, distorts and inflames. It *can* wreak havoc, and one way is to disallow conclusions made in it about each other's character.

2. Staying away from generalising about the particulars – e.g., not bringing past arguments and misdemeanours into present arguments: 'And another thing . . . That's just like the time before' or 'And it's not the first time you've made me feel like this: you did this and that and this and that . . .' You quickly get into character assassination this way: 'You *always* do this', etc.

174

3. Refraining from 'reading the other's mind': 'I know what you're like, and I know why you are doing this.' Most of the time, even though you do know each other very well, you are wrong, because you have lost the sense of your partner as your ally by this time and have turned him or her into a virtually unrecognisable ogre. You might be right about the ogre, but not at all right about your partner.

4. Avoiding a defensive stance: denying responsibility, making excuses, putting it back on to your partner. 'Well, I only did that because you did X'/'I did not do that; it's just your perception that's wrong'; trying to minimise or detour the discussion from any criticism of you: 'Yes, but . . .' or 'That's not the point. You did X to me!'

The primitive response to blame and criticism is denial of responsibility. The mature response is to face up to it, weigh the evidence, and see if it fits. If it does, there is usually a way to make amends, often simply by validating the complainant's point, apologising, and offering to do something to make it right (although sometimes what's done is done, and only the first two steps are either possible or necessary). Denial fans the flames. Yet so many of us so much of the time do anything rather than admit guilt, let alone apologise. One reason is there is a demon, in the form of something called a 'catastrophic fear', governing all of us. We are afraid of something really terrible, from a sense of shame to real retribution for our crimes. But usually we don't know what that demon is, and through naming it, we can stare it down. When our partners criticise us, the demon is usually something to do with the fear that we will be rejected: faulty goods, not lovable any more. Facing that demon usually dispels it because, especially if caught early enough, it usually isn't true. In fact, accepting criticism, acknowledging the other's position or feelings, is usually enough to heal the breach in loving feelings.

5. Avoiding recriminations (i.e. baggage from past anger, which distorts): 'You deserve what you get!' See what has already been said about anger – it applies here, too.

6. Sticking to the particular; avoiding dragging past mis-behaviours into a specific complaint. It is almost impossible to be constructive in a dispute if the complaints are general: who can or would want to try to fix their whole character or change all their bad habits? Instead, it can be very enabling to feel that you have chosen a small thing which you can work on together, fix it and move on. A great sense of optimism prevails, and the next disagreement does not loom so ominously. For instance, telling your partner how he hurt your feelings when he did not comment on your make-over hairdo, although everyone else, from your next-door-neighbour to the shop assistant at the corner shop did, and then getting both a compliment and apology is a lot easier than building it up into, 'You never compliment me. You never even notice. Last time I got my hair cut, and the time before, and the time before that you never said a thing, but so and so told me I looked beautiful!'

7. Countering assaults with apologies: as no couples are perfect, all will probably at some point, especially during a downward spiral, enter into some of the above behaviour. Moreover, many couples do get into a cycle of blame and anger; in a downward spiral criticism becomes a key feeling about your partner. You begin to criticise over and over. When you do any of these things, a basic ground rule is one of civil behaviour in general: apologise. Make amends. Show gratitude. Then be patient, as the hurt dissolves. These approaches can be like magic pills, erasing black moods, sometimes (but certainly not always) instantly.

Other couples have their own specific ground rules, such as not mentioning Great Aunt Mollie who insulted your partner's mother at the wedding. One **exercise** to try is for both of you separately to make a list of what you each think are the basic ground rules of your relationship. Then compare them. Compare them to the ones above, and see if you can come up with a compatible list between you.

b. 'Time-out'

When small children have tantrums many parents give them 'time-out': time in their room, or in the corner, in which they are to cool down. The same is true for adults. When emotions run high we cannot think straight, tend to fly off the handle and often say and do things which are expedient but hurtful. No one is perfect in controlling such impulses, but once these take control or threaten to do so, 'time-out' is indicated. Remove yourself from the catalyst – your partner – until 1. both of you have calmed down, and 2. both feel they can think through the problem from both points of view. This is a strategy which men who batter their wives are always told is a bottom-line technique. It also applies to hot emotions. Agreeing to this *beforehand* as a strategy will help both members of the couple, should tempers become heated. At this point, both partners are ready to try to reinterpret the other's behaviour, and so to begin to try to employ tracking, reframing, empathy and insight.

Again, this is a strategy which research on conflict management in general, and in marriages, in particular, has demonstrated is effective[2]. Time-out is about calming down. In time-out, heart rate and blood pressure settle down, and the flight or flight response which overrules the ability to think well recedes, for you have removed yourself from the stimulus which is activating them. John Gottmann's research on marital conflict[3] suggests learning some simple calming down techniques, such as relaxation exercises, which restore normal breathing, and hence blood pressure and heart rates.

c. Clear and direct communication:

Anyone who has been on a communications training course for work has been taught the basic point that the clearer you are in expressing what you need and what you mean, the better will be your chances for getting what you want. A corollary is that you are more likely to get what you want if you express yourself clearly to the appropriate person. Redirecting communication through a third party usually distorts and takes it ultimately out of your control.

What is true for the workplace is doubly true in intimate relations, where there are more opportunities for unclear and indirect communications to occur. A set of studies by therapists[4] has successfully demonstrated the usefulness of these precepts. Families who do well, especially in family therapy, are those in which, among other qualities, communications between members are both direct and clear.

What this implies is that each partner has to *take responsibility for stating his or her needs, thoughts, feelings and desires, if he or she wants the other to know them.* Too often we assume that true love and intimacy means that our partners should be able to read our minds. Doing so and getting it right is seen as the equivalent of loving behaviour. But as we have seen, especially when couples feel emotionally estranged or angry at each other, they are least able to intuit what their partner is thinking. Their anger distorts their images of each other. Moreover, even in the most focused and protective couple, partners get it wrong, or can be otherwise engaged, not focusing on the partner's needs. Finally, in any couple there are conflicts of interest which override the ability to see the other's point from the outset.

All this argues for the importance of not relying on your partner to guess and read your thoughts. Instead, the responsibility falls on each member to state, not wait. It is fortuitous and time-saving when words are not needed, but not to be expected as the norm.

An **exercise** to try, which might be revealing, is to try to remember the last time you made a difficult request of your partner which caused an argument (this could have been a request for help, or information, or for a change in his or her behaviour, for instance). Can you remember how you phrased the request? Did you give the rationale from your point of view for it? Did you put yourself in his or her shoes first to think about the effect of the request on him or her? Did you ask for it in a timely manner, or wait, expecting him or her to 'read your mind' and then, when that failed, in some anger, hurt, or resentment, finally state what you wanted?

As many researchers on communications, conflict resolution, and marital therapists studying effective marital communications have found, clear communications start with 'I' statements: 'I felt such and such' or 'I wondered if this is what you meant' or 'I did such and such because' both means that you are taking responsibility for your perceptions, actions and feelings, and also does not presume that you know what goes on in your partner's mind. 'Such and such about you makes me do X' or 'You always want Y' will predictably put your partner on the defensive and render him or her less likely to listen to you. And as we have seen, by the time resentments have entered the relationship you have probably got it wrong about your partner, and vice versa, anyway. 'I' statements serve to curtail misperceptions and misattributions about your partner's behaviour and his or hers about your own.

Think back to a recent disagreement between you and your partner. Can you remember how your partner phrased his or her criticisms or accusations? How you phrased yours? If it got out of hand, it is most likely that you both used accusatory, rather than 'I', statements. How could you have phrased your complaint with an 'I' statement? How could your partner have phrased his or hers?

The study on marital conflict styles which is discussed in Chapter 4 identifies 'non-defensive' statements as key in getting marriages back on course after conflict. Defensive statements on one side breed defensive statements on the other side. 'I' statements are, by definition, non-defensive – they are not about accusing, but about assuming some (not necessarily all) personal responsibility. In turn, they imply an invitation for the other to examine his own portion of responsibility for the conflict.

Direct communications also stem potentially spiralling distortions. Instead of telling your husband's sister about how he hurt your feelings, with the hope that she will set him right, it is usually much less risky to find the right, clear way to let him know directly. After all, his sister may come at him with the full force of all the times he insulted her during their childhood, which may inflate the issue out of proportion. Or she may downplay it out of loyalty, distorting it in the other direction. Or she may administer recurring jibes like a Chinese water torture, continuing long after your squabble with him is over. Once in her hands it is out of yours.

James and Valerie achieved empathy and reframed, gained insight and employed the various behavioural steps, from tracking to establishing ground rules and time-out, and finally began communicating directly and clearly to each other. This turned their relationship around, but, as the next chapter argues, unless they had gone on to enact the rest of the five factors the upward spiral would not have been maintained.

CHAPTER TWELVE

Focus, Gratitude, Balance and Pleasure: Making Them Happen

To change a downward into an upward spiral, couples must enact all five factors.

The strategies described in the previous chapter indicate some ways for increasing protectiveness between you. They also apply to setting the scene for enacting the other factors. But there are additional methods to employ, and this chapter will describe them, for each factor.

1. Focus

Focus means giving attention, energy and time to each other.

James and Valerie further enacted a change in behaviour by each *focusing* on each other: instead of spending a morning privately obsessing over how he was going to manage to conceal his contact with his ex-wife from Valerie, not to mention how he was going to manage his telephone conversation with her so that he wouldn't antagonise her, James was free to discuss his dilemma with Valerie. In fact, once he had been open with her about his fears of losing her and his children she became his ally. She became adept at creating background noises to indicate (imaginary) friends who had just arrived, or emergency needs for the phone, which helped James to end difficult conversations with his ex. He could freely get off the phone and vent his frustration with her to Valerie, who listened sympathetically. She focused on him. But James was also focusing on Valerie by thinking about how she would have felt if he'd carried on secretly. This freed each in other ways to be attentive to the other. As resentment abated they positively wanted to spend time and energy on each other. Thus this one small change – sharing the burden of the phone contact – set into motion other changes of focused time and attention.

In order to prevent any wedges growing between Valerie and James's children, the couple nominated some activities they could all pleasurably share together, thereby increasing time spent together over the access weekends. One evening was spent either going for a meal or getting a video, or going bowling or to the cinema. But in order to preserve a space for the couple, this meant that on the alternate weekends, as well as at least once during the week (so a comfortable balance between family and couple life is achieved) the couple nominated something they would do together, which also felt as if they were doing something special. As they had already taken salsa dancing lessons, they chose to go dancing one night. More than that, they made sure that they routinely ate together each evening, even though some evenings one of them had a late appointment. During meals the TV was off, reading matter was banned and the answer machine on. The couple were forced to talk, and soon talk became easy and pleasurable. Focus was not very difficult to achieve.

There are some strategies and **exercises** for achieving more focus on each other. Prioritising is one such strategy.

Prioritising time together

Who has not felt in our marriages or partnerships that we

are being taken for granted? Dailiness and reliability are the main culprits. The very comfort of being able to be relaxed in the presence of our loved ones gives us the licence to behave in unwittingly hurtful ways. Not making time and space for our partners delivers the implicit message that other things are more important. A steady diet of being last on the list and never being given time or pride of place corrodes anyone's sense of importance.

The exercise of going over how much time has been spent together, when and doing what over the past month, or two months, or three, or six, extending into a year, perhaps, can be very revealing. (Diaries are essential here in jogging memories.) If both members of the couple do this and find that they both come up with less than regular, consistent and well-spent time together, this is diagnostic of a relationship which needs more focus; if you are not already in trouble you will be. Having made this time diagnosis you can be on the way to changing the quality of the relationship dramatically, as did James and Valerie.

But this change takes a change in priorities first, and second, a clear commitment to spending a regular (e.g., one evening a week minimum, especially at first, if you feel you are already in trouble) amount of time together. It may mean writing down the planned time together in diaries as a fixed appointment, which nothing subverts (apart from illness or the like). This demonstrates the change in priorities, with the relationship moving to the top at the times specified, and the commitment to the new regime indicating its movement up, in general. This is what James and Valerie were doing in selecting an evening in which they went dancing.

Setting aside regular, focused time together

In addition, a regular daily time in which you spend time together on your own can also be key in developing more focus. In this time you can return to any issues which need further discussion, or you can divest yourselves of the day's trivia, perhaps through a daily recounting of what you've done, respectively, or catch up on other events (such as talks with teachers, or reports from children or what the children did while the other parent was not present), or you can get frustrations off your chests. Usually this time can be mixed with other things, such as reading together, or listening to music, but I have found that at the beginning of trying this, couples have to be strict with specifying a proportion, at the beginning, for talking, much of which may feel extremely stilted at first. Developing a comfortable style of talking takes time, but almost always develops with persistence. Some couples take this time over dinner together, especially if they do not have children (or do not eat with them). Others do it in a specially designated half-hour or so before bed-time, over a cup of something or a glass of wine. Turning off the television, and not answering the phone during this time is important, as it was for James and Valerie. Otherwise your focus is diffuse. Over time, some of these strictures may be eased, so that the half-hour can include more listening to music, or can take brief interruptions from phones and children, for instance. But a couple needs to get into the habit of this kind of intimacy, and establishing new habits takes time. In time they come to expect it of each other and it then comes more naturally.

Setting boundaries

One reason for setting clear time together is that it puts *boundaries* around you, the couple: a prohibition against taking phone calls tells your partner, as well as the outside world, that the outside world will not intrude on you, the couple. A whole body of work in family therapy has been based in part around the notion of the importance of setting boundaries around the different subgroups of the family (for example, around the generations, in particular, and most importantly, around the couple)[1]. Closing the door or otherwise closing off a space lets the children know that when Mum and Dad are in the sitting room at 10.00 p.m. with the door closed, this is the parents' time together. It also models for children that it is important in adult love relationships to commit time and attention. Without boundaries around the couple family life gets skewed. The couple gets lost in the process, the children become over-strong, and communication within the couple unit becomes attenuated and usually distorted as a result.

Putting such boundaries around a couple through the commitment of time and activities together may mean chang-ing the rules and practices of many families. Children may not immediately conform, and best friends and in-laws used to phoning in the evenings at the time when the couple has chosen to meet may persist in phoning. As with any change, with a strong commitment to the new behaviour, as demon-strated by sticking to it, the system around you also eventually changes and adapts.

2. Gratitude

Gratitude means demonstrating appreciation and acknow-ledging your partner's value to you.

Gratitude was achieved for Valerie and James in part through the therapist pointing out to the other just what each one's efforts to aid the partner had been. Therapy thereby made each conscious of how much the other had worked to change and how much was already in place between them but had gone unnoticed. Acknowledging how much they appreciated the other's efforts came as a consequence of noticing them.

Valerie and James continued this expression outside the therapist's office. After the first access weekend following their successful contact negotiations, when all had gone swimmingly, James presented Valerie with a bunch of flowers.

She hugged him in appreciation, and thanked him for doing something which had been hard for him (that is, cutting the phone contact short). This appreciation eventually got expressed habitually non-verbally. When James had his phone contact and completed it within a short space of time, Valerie gave him an affectionate gesture, a peck on the cheek, a squeeze of the hand, in acknowledgement of his effort. A smile from him, in return, sealed the appreciation with balance. Similarly, when James came into a neat bedroom after a difficult day he thanked Valerie, since he knew that tidiness was not as automatic for her as for him, and a tidy bedroom represented an effort she had made for him. Valerie also thanked him for being punctilious about using the message pad she ostentatiously put next to the telephone.

Getting into habits of expressing and receiving gratitude

For James and Valerie gratitude was sometimes expressed verbally ('Thank you for tidying up the room') but sometimes through non-verbal acknowledgements. The point was one partner recognised an appreciation or sense of gratitude when it was expressed by the other.

In the beginning, especially for couples who have lost their way and settled into habits of bad behaviour and attributions of poor motives towards each other, explicitly expressing thank-you's verbally is indicated. If you are in a downward spiral, a commitment to change the habit, reversing non-gratitude and criticism into expressed thanks, admiration and appreciation needs to be made. This is in part because such clarity vitiates the need to argue about whether something was appreciated or not. Communication becomes clear. Make the commitment to do this for a reasonable amount of time: too short and the habit won't be changed; too long and it will feel impossible to do. Try doing it first for a week, then renewing the commitment weekly. Over enough weeks the habit should feel both more ingrained, and also the spiral should be on its way up, making it easier to express appreciative feelings.

Expressing thanks or acknowledging positive things about your partner throughout the week will feel stilted. Many people protest at this suggestion ('What? You mean I have to thank her for cooking the meal? Why don't I thank her for buying the toilet paper which has enabled me to wipe my bottom?') Guidelines for when to thank, at the point of marital disaffection, are not difficult to establish. You return to accepted rules of courtesy as for strangers: these have usually lapsed to the point of discourtesy in warring partners. Most people can recognise when a partner has made a special effort and, under a commitment to new rules of courtesy, frequently can become more demonstrative in their appreciation. But such recognition is not infallible. Sometimes it takes the person making the effort to flag that the effort has been made. If a special meal has been cooked but nice meals are the norm, your partner may not realise you have gone to any unusual lengths. 'Did you like that soup – it was a new recipe I spent some time over' flags that it was a special case.

As a couple becomes more used to noticing each other's efforts and more habitually expresses thanks, the modes of this expression can become more relaxed and varied. James and Valerie eventually moved to non-verbal cues such as appreciative smiles and hugs. Sometimes gratitude is demonstrated through a gift or by a reciprocal effort – an errand run as a favour in return for a favour done. Trust in the other's benevolence towards you can expand the repertoire of what you and your partner encode as gratitude. What should become habitual is punctuation of special efforts on the other's behalf, be it through some verbal or non-verbal gesture.

3. Balance

Balance means a reciprocal, mutual give and take.

As we know, all the efforts one person makes at protection, focus and gratitude are in the end usually ground down to nothing if they are one-sided. They need to be balanced, or near-balanced, to work. Rewards, in the form of actions in kind for efforts made, reinforce such behaviour and make it much more likely to recur, as mountains of psychological studies attest. There are some strategies which are extremely effective, and even essential to do for getting the balance right and the following **exercises** describe these.

Assuming responsibility

The only way to ensure the occurrence of balance is to assume responsibility for the enactment of the factors yourself. If each partner undertakes this responsibility, for the duration of the relationship, there is already, by definition, balance. If each waits for the other to respond in kind until taking the next action most relationships will founder on the unbalanced foundations.

Responsibility and communication

This is where direct and clear communication come very much to the fore. Because as we have noted in Chapter 3 men and women often do not interpret the same behaviours in the same way, each may not be noting the other's efforts. For example, as discussed in Chapter 2, research shows that men commonly complain that they go out of their way to help their wives by fixing things around the house, yet wives do not perceive them as helpful, while wives lodge similar complaints against their husbands. Feeling that you are doing all of the running is, in most couples, a distortion most of the time; however, it is a sense usually fed by muteness about what you are doing, on the one hand, and unexpressed appreciation from your partner, on the other. The obvious way into this conundrum is twofold: 1. to get into habits of expressing appreciation, as discussed above, and 2. to point out what efforts you have been making, and request ones you would be helped by, in return. In the section in the previous chapter on clear and direct communication, and also in the one on 'I' statements, are some guidelines for how to state such things clearly and appropriately.

In the midst of Valerie's complaints about James's disrespect and insensitivity to her insecurity, she complained that he was consistently unhelpful to her. He would come home and flop on the chair while she cooked, exhausted herself after a full working day. Enraged, James unleashed a litany of his contributions, ending with, 'And who, tell me, *who* spent all of my one free day last Sunday looking for a place to copy your report, then who took it in, bound it, and who sent it off for you the next morning?' Valerie barely missed a beat before starting to disqualify him, claiming that all of that was 'easy for James, it was part of the kind of stuff he does at work every day.' Seeing his shocked and hurt expression, she backed down and was forced to re-evaluate her picture of him as 'unhelpful'. Reframing it as 'James helping in the ways he does best' moved Valerie further towards accepting him, acknowledging what he does do for her, rather than focusing on what he does not. Gratitude for what James does for her then came more easily.

In this example James took the initiative in stating what he did do. This clarified to Valerie what he felt were the special efforts for which he wanted acknowledgement. Without it she went on assuming that these efforts were not special ('It's what he does every day'). James made a clear and direct 'I' statement, and then Valerie could reframe his actions and give them proper acknowledgement.

4. Pleasure

Pleasure means enjoying your marriage and delighting in each other.

James and Valerie's experienced pleasure in each other grew enormously, increased through their proactive enactment of the other factors. More often than not, they laughed and smiled in each other's company, thought of each other affectionately when each was not with the other, and wanted to be in the other's presence. This was in contrast to previously, when each had spent a lot of time and effort avoiding the other, either in trepidation of an outburst or stewing in resentment. Through what was at first self-conscious behaviour, habits changed. What had been labelled negatively before became labelled with generosity now: 'selfish and uncaring' became 'unwittingly preoccupied by fear and pain'. This couple became the loving partnership they had meant to be.

As an **exercise** in increasing pleasure, you might try some of what James and Valerie did. That is, they reframed their idea of pleasure by breaking it down into its component bits. In this way they did not demand the earth of each other, or that the relationship deliver Pleasure-with-a-Capital-P. By scaling down their expectations they also relieved the strain that their marriage be perfect and allowed them to focus on what was indeed pleasurable. In this new frame, the sense of pleasure grew.

They did this by:
1. Catching thoughts and statements about deprivation – that is, thoughts and statements like: 'I never get' or 'You never do'. These are ideas which focus on what the relationship is not delivering.
2. Replacing these thoughts with new ones which emphasise the particular contributions their partner makes. It is imperative that as soon as the negative deprivation thought appears it is actively replaced with the new one.

This requires a good deal of effort, especially at first, until it becomes habitual. One technique for helping this to occur is to write a list, when you are feeling relatively positive about your partner, of a number of positive contributions he or she makes to your life. Then, when a negative, deprivation thought occurs, take a piece of paper. On one side write the negative, deprivation thoughts. Next to it, write down one of the counter-positive ones. Keep this list handy so you can use it when a new negative thought erupts.

3. Take the list of pleasurable behaviours, and try to add to them, as they occur, to your list of positive counter-statements (such as 'He showed delight in me – he smiled in delight when we met unexpectedly in the street on Thursday'). In this way the focus on what has been pleasurably experienced together begins to replace the focus on what has not.

A word about the need for marital therapy

Valerie and James were helped by being in therapy, in large part because they had lost their way, and the therapist sign-posted it for them. But couples do not necessarily need a third, professional party to get back on track. Following these steps – insight into vulnerability, taking the behavioural steps towards becoming more protective, and then proactively enacting the five factors through a self-conscious change in behaviour and attributions towards one's partner – is possible for many without therapy. Catching things early is helpful. There is a better prognosis for improvement without therapy before resentment has turned into a brick wall of contempt between you. Once the wall is up and the memories of affection and good-will seem like distant flickers, therapy is almost certainly indicated: the habits of bad marital behaviour and wrong attributions have become so ingrained that it may be impossible to think your own way out of them.

CONCLUSION

There Are Second Chances in Love

In the end, we all want to have relationships like Harry and Rose's. Married for forty years, they recently went to South Africa for a three-week holiday to visit their daughter who lives there. Told that the flight would be long, perhaps eleven hours, Harry brightened. 'Oh, boy,' he said to his daughter, 'that means I get your mother all to myself, right next to me, for all that time!' He meant it. Or, to be able to say, 'Well, darling, hasn't it been a long and happy time together?' as one famous playwright said to his wife of fifty years, as he lay dying. To walk the road, however rocky, together and with happiness, is a privilege which more of us should, and hopefully can, have.

The five couples whose stories predominate in this book – Jackie and Obi, Nina and John, Irene and John, Iona and Joe and Mark and Margaret – are all both ordinary and extra-ordinary. Ordinary in the details of their lives, extraordinary in the generous and patient way they love each other. Each has turned a trial or tribulation into a time to forge a deeper connection through metaphorically rushing to each other's side at the (again metaphorical) alarm bell. Some of the men were initially resistant and even they concede that to choose to stay with the partner with whom they fell in love, to honour that love through the work of commitment, has made them fortunate, more fortunate than others with more money or position.

Thinking of the destruction, the debris of their friends' broken relationships around them, Iona shakes her head sadly as we gaze at her impossibly young and radiant image staring out at us from her 33-year-old black-and-white wedding album. 'It's really terrible, really sad. You know we all started out the same, in love and hopeful, thinking we'd be married forever.' She sighs. 'Joe and I are the only ones left. I'm sure they loved each other, but we've been the only lucky ones.'

It is not luck, though. It is work and dedication and knowing that the reward of that investment are times of marvel and pleasure and that, yes, there's another person on this earth who hears your voice, in its distress and in its delight, and comes. As this chapter heading says, there can be second (and third and fourth) chances in the game of love. As these couples testify, it is well worth trying.

NOTES

Introduction

1. The best research up to this point (Blumstein, P., and Schwartz, P., *American Couples*, Pocket Books, New York, 1983; Haskey, J., 'Trends in Marriage and Cohabitation: The Decline in Marriage and the Changing Pattern of Living in Partnerships', *Population Trends, no. 80*, Summer 1995; Nick Buck and Jacqueline Scott, in a talk entitled 'New Evidence on Cohabitation Spells from the British Household Panel Study', which was delivered to the Marriage and Divorce Seminar Group, 5 July 1995) suggests that cohabitations which survive over many years are not different from marriage in any notable respect: they apparently have the same rules regarding fidelity, joint ownership of essentials and a commitment to live in the future together. This similarity is particularly true when there are children.

2. Reibstein, J., and Richards, M., *Sexual Arrangements: Marriage, Monogamy and Affairs*, Heinemann, London, 1992.

Part One

Chapter 1

1. Kiernan, K. E., and Estangh, V., *Cohabitation*, Family Policies Study Centre, London, 1993.

2. *c.f.* Cuber, J. F., and Haroff, P., *The Significant Americans: A Study of Sexual Behaviour Among the Affluent*, Appleton-Century, New York, 1965; also Blumstein and Schwartz, *American Couples*, Pocket Books, New York, 1983; also Beavers, R., in *Successful Marriage: A Family Systems Approach to Couples Therapy*, W. W. Norton and Co, London and New York, 1985; and Maggie Scarf's *Intimate Partners*, Century, London, 1987.

3. Research on marital satisfaction is well summarised in Dr Jack

Dominian's book, *Marriage: the Definitive Guide to What Makes a Marriage Work*, Heinemann, London, 1995.

4. For example, Harville Hendrix's *Getting the Love You Want*, Harper Perennial, New York, 1988.

Chapter 2

1. As postulated by John Bowlby, which derives from a Darwinian view of love, that it is necessary and functional for the species. See, for instance, Bowlby, J., *Attachment and Loss: Vol.One: Attachment*, Basic Books, New York, 1969.

2. It need not be simply mothers, as even Bowlby conceded near the end of his life.

3. Erich Fromm, in his cult classic, *The Art of Loving*, Thorsons, London, 1995, is the main culprit of this.

4. See Dr Jack Dominian's *Marriage: the Definitive Guide to What Makes a Marriage Work*, Heinemann, London, 1995.

5. See, for example, Carol Gilligan, *In a Different Voice*, Harvard University Press, Cambridge, Mass., 1982; Reibstein, J., and Richards, M., *Sexual Arrangements: Marriage, Monogamy and Affairs*, Heinemann, London, 1992; Chodorow, N., *The Reproduction of Mothering*, University of California Press, Berkeley, 1978.

6. See Cancian, F., *Love in America: Gender and Self-Development*, Cambridge University Press, Cambridge, 1987.

7. See Giddens, A., *The Transformation of Intimacy*, Polity, Cambridge, 1992, for a discussion of this.

8. Cancian, *op. cit.*

9. *Ibid.*

Chapter 3

1. The language of object relations and ego psychology spoken by clinicians, healers, and theorists which has dominated Western psychology for the last half-century, becomes outmoded. This language pervades most books and studies of marriage. In them we meet two separate but hopefully equal individuals, reaching out across both their separateness and the wounds of their broken relationships (wounds derived from relationships with their mothers and fathers) who must heal these either through love (for instance, as in Harville Hendrix's *Getting the Love*

You Want, (Harper Perennial, New York, 1988), or else heal and then love (see, for instance, Erik Erikson in *Childhood and Society*, W.W. Norton and Co., New York, 1963); or Erich Fromm (*The Art of Loving*, Thorsons, London, 1995).

2. See Cancian, F., *Love in America: Gender and Self-Development*, Cambridge University Press, Cambridge, 1987.

3. Carol Gilligan, for instance, looked at the way women resolve thorny moral problems in contrast to men. In her study, *In a Different Voice*, (Harvard University Press, Cambridge, Mass., 1982), she reports her finding that the principles women bring to bear on their solutions to these problems are always to do with consequences upon others' lives, or with their sense of responsibility for how their actions and decisions affect others. In contrast, her then colleague at Harvard, the psychologist Lawrence Kohlberg, who had studied moral reasoning before Gilligan, found that men used abstract moral principles, such as 'for the higher good of mankind'. Others who write out of this 'relational psychology' perspective include Jean Baker Miller (*Toward a New Psychology of Women*, Beacon Press, Boston, 1986); Mary Jo Belencky and her co-authors (*Women's Ways of Knowing*, Basic Books, New York, 1986); Judith Herman's work on the effect of trauma on women (*Trauma and Recovery*, Basic Books, New York, 1992), to name a few of the most prominent.

4. See Cancian, F., *Love in America: Gender and Self-Development*, Cambridge University Press, Cambridge, 1987 for a discussion of this and list of references on the subject.

5. See Deborah Tannen, *'You Just Don't Understand'*, Virago, London, 1991, and others, such as John Gray, in *Men, Women, and Relationships*, Beyond Words Publishing, Hillsboro, Oregon, 1993.

6. This was first described by John Bowlby, but much elaborated upon since by others in increasingly sophisticated studies of the emotional attachments people make, not just during infancy, but over the whole life cycle. (See, for instance, *The Psychology of Love*, edited by R. Sternberg and M. Barnes, Yale University Press, New Haven, 1988; or Colin Murray Parkes and Joan Stevenson-Hinde's *The Place of Attachment in Human Behaviour*, Tavistock Publications, London, 1982.

7. In particular, the work of psychologists such as Robert Weiss (see his 'Attachment in Adult Life' (in Murray Parkes and Stevenson-Hinde, *ibid.*) and also of Shaver and his colleagues (see the article entitled 'Love as Attachment' in Sternberg and Barnes, *op.cit.*) have documented the similarities of behaviours between loving adults and parents and children, and the similarities of the functions of both kinds of secure and important relationships.

8. *Further notes*:
   a. The centrality of a sense of safety, value and security to the experience of love is shown in a recent article in *The New York Review of Books* by the literary critic, Rosemary Dinnage. In reviewing Pat Barker's trilogy which ends with the Booker Prize-winning *The Ghost Road*, Dinnage describes a central character in all three novels, the anthropologist/psychiatrist, Rivers. 'He was loved,' she writes. 'Sassoon wrote that "there was never any doubt about my liking him. *He made me feel safe at once* and seemed to know all about me" . . .' (Feb 15, 1996, p.19; my italics).
   b. 'Protection' as a focal point in successful love has been written about and around by most people who talk about either love or marital satisfaction. It is what is pointed to by John Gottmann in *Why Marriages Succeed or Fail* (Simon and Schuster, New York, 1994) when he talks about the need to be empathic, which helps to avert conflict or to soothe rows when they erupt; by Ethel Spector Person (*Dreams of Love and Fateful Encounters: The Power of Romantic Passion*, Penguin, New York, 1988) when she discusses the romantic merger which fuels love; by Erich Fromm (*The Art of Loving*, Thorsons, London, 1995) who described forcefully that need to merge and to feel as if you are one with your lover; and the researchers on love and attachment in adulthood referred to earlier (see especially *The Psychology of Love*, edited by Robert Sternberg and Michael Barnes, Yale University Press, New Haven, 1988).

Chapter 4

1. Zeldin, T., in *An Intimate History of Humanity* (Minerva, London, 1994) makes this point.
2. See the studies in particular by Epstein, N., et al., from Canada on communication patterns in families, particularly in family therapy (as, for instance in Epstein, N., et al. 'The McMaster Model of Family Functioning,' *Journal of Marriage and Family Counselling*, 1978, *4*, pp.19-31).
3. See, for instance, D. W. Winnicott's *The Maturational Processes and the Facilitating Environment: Studies in the Theory of Emotional Development*, The Hogarth Press and the Institute of Psychoanalysis, London, 1982.
4. John Gottmann summarises these findings from his research in his very useful study of marital interactions, *Why Marriages Succeed or Fail*, Simon and Schuster, New York, 1994.
5. See a discussion of this in Reibstein, J., and Richards, M., *Sexual Arrangements: Marriage, Monogamy and Affairs*, Heinemann, London, 1992.
6. *Ibid.*
7. *Ibid.*

Chapter 5

1. See Theodore Zeldin's *An Intimate History of Humanity*, Minerva, London, 1994.
2. See Hicks, M., and Platt, M., 'Marital Happiness and Stability: A Review of Research in the Sixties', *Journal of Marriage and the Family*, vol. 32, pp. 553-574, London, 1970. Also see Wallerstein, J., and Kelly, J., *Surviving the Breakup*, Basic Books, New York, 1980; and Burgoyne, J., Ormrod, R., and Richards, M., *Divorce Matters*, Penguin Books, Harmondsworth, 1987.
3. See Epstein, N., et al., 'The McMaster Model of Family Functioning'. In Walsh, F. (ed.), *Normal Family Processes*, Guilford, New York, 1982.
4. See, for instance, Ainsworth, M., et al., *Patterns of Attachment: A Psychological Study of the Strange Situation*, Hillsdale, N. J., Lawrence Erlbaum, 1978.
5. See Robert Weiss (pp. 171-184) in Murray Parkes, C., and Stevenson-Hinde, J., *The Place of Attachment in Human*

Behaviour, Tavistock Publications, London, 1982.
6. See Dr Jack Dominian's book, *Marriage: The Definitive Guide to What Makes a Marriage Work* (Heinemann, London, 1995) for a review of this research.

Chapter 6

1. See Melanie Klein in 'The Early Stages of the Oedipal Conflict', *International Journal of Psychoanalysis*, 1928-9, pp. 167–180; also her book, *The Psychoanalysis of Children*, Hogarth Press, London, 1932; and Klein, M., and Riviere, J., *Love, Hate and Reparation*, W. W. Norton, New York, 1964.

Chapter 7

General note: In his book *Marriage: The Definitive Guide to What Makes a Marriage Work*, (Heinemann, London, 1995) Dr Jack Dominian writes that part of what research has suggested characterises happy couples is that they express admiration and appreciation for each other. John Gottmann's research (*Why Marriages Succeed or Fail*, Simon and Schuster, New York, 1994) finds that validation is key to couples being able to mend conflicts and feel happy together. Some of what is meant by 'validation' is praise, admiration, and the expression of appreciation. Balance is also pointed to by such qualities as mutuality (see, for instance, the discussion in Gottmann for the need to be mutual in heading off rising marital discord).

1. See Klein, M., and Riviere, J., *Love, Hate and Reparation*, W.W. Norton, New York, 1964.
2. Benedek, T., 'Parenthood as a Developmental Phase', *Journal of the American Psychoanalytic Association*, 7, no. 3, pp. 389–417, 1959.
3. See Cancian, F., *Love in America: Gender and Self-Development*, Cambridge University Press, Cambridge, 1987.
4. Gray, John, *Men are from Mars, Women are from Venus*, HarperCollins, London, 1993.

Chapter 8

Pleasure is pointed to by authors such as Erich Fromm, *The Art of Loving*, Thorsons, London, 1995; Gottmann, J., *Why Marriages*

Succeed or Fail, Simon and Schuster, New York, 1994; Person, *Dreams of Love and Fateful Encounters: The Power of Romantic Passion*, Penguin, New York, 1988. They talk of qualities such as enjoyment, sexual pleasure, eroticism, shared sense of humour, mutual enjoyment; a shared narrative – and the prospect of the shared narrative and history.

Theodore Zeldin's discussion of the importance of humour and enjoyment in intimacy (*An Intimate History of Humanity*, Minerva, London, 1994) also points to a similar emphasis on pleasure in intimate relationships.

Part Two

Chapter 9

1. See, for example, how Eric Fromm, in his writing about how people try to maintain love, once they've fallen in love, in the classic treatise, *The Art of Loving*, (Thorsons, London, 1995) describes how people introject a 'fatherly conscience', through which they modify behaviour in order to become more lovable and acceptable. Similarly, in John Gottmann's study of marriages which work, *Why Marriages Succeed or Fail*, (Simon and Schuster, New York, 1994) he stresses that it is within couples' interactions with each other that improvement of poor relationships can come – i.e., a couple can work on making things better by changing their interactions.

Chapter 10

1. See Betty Carter and Monica McGoldrick, (eds.) *The Family Life Cycle: A Framework for Family Therapy*, Gardner Press, New York, 1980.
2. Froma Walsh (see particularly her edited volume, *Normal Family Processes*, Guilford, New York, 1982) is a noted family therapist who has described these points.
3. See Cowan, C., and Cowan, P., *When Partners Become Parents: The Big Life Change for Couples*, Basic Books, New York, 1992.
4. See Reibstein, J., and Richards, M., *Sexual Arrangements: Marriage, Monogamy and Affairs*, (Heinemann, London, 1992) for a further discussion of this.
5. Gail Sheehy talked about this in her bestseller of the 1970's,

Passages, (Bantam, New York, 1976) and Angela Neustatter, in her new book on middle age and ageing, *Look the Demon in the Eye: The Challenge of Mid-life* (Michael Joseph, London, 1996) tells a number of striking stories of men and women who are beginning to think this way about their lives. Terri Apter, in her study of women in their forties and fifties, *Secret Paths*, (W. W. Norton, London, 1995) does as well.

6. See Reibstein and Richards, *op. cit.*

Chapter 11

1. This is based on a model pioneered by The Chicago Centre for Family Studies/The Family Institute (with work by William Pinsof and others, and which itself is a fusion of psychoanalytic ideas and research conducted at McMasters University).
2. Reframing is a technique widely used in family therapy, and developed mainly by those working in what is known as a strategic model. For a discussion and list of relevant references on reframing see Simon, F., et al., *The Language of Family Therapy: A Systemic Vocabulary and Sourcebook*, The Family Process Press, New York, 1985.
3. Other studies of successful marriages underscore this point. Among these, for instance, are John Gottmann's study (*Why Marriages Succeed or Fail*, Simon and Schuster, New York, 1994) in which it is revealed how sticking to ground rules was part of the way the successful couples managed their conflicts; Maggie's Scarfe's couples in her book *Intimate Partners* (Century, London, 1987) similarly reported the importance of feeling safe within these acknowledged boundaries. Gottmann's study pinpoints the need for 'calming down' techniques in general.
4. Most famously, this is shown in research carried out by groups based at McMasters University in Canada (c.f., Epstein, N., et al., 'The McMaster Model of Family Functioning', *Journal of Marriage and Family Counselling*, 1978, *4*, pp. 19-31).

Chapter 12

1. See, for instance, Minuchin, S., *Families and Family Therapy*, Tavistock, London, 1974.

About the Author

Janet Reibstein, PhD, is a long-married psychologist and psychotherapist, with two sons, who has practised and taught on both sides of the Atlantic for many years. She works primarily with couples. She is the author of the book, *Sexual Arrangements: Marriage and the Temptation of Infidelity* (in the US); *Sexual Arrangements: Marriage, Monogamy and Affairs* (in the UK and Australia), a study of affairs and marriage (co-authored with Martin Richards). She is the author of numerous articles on marriage, in both the popular press and in academic journals and books.

She is also a frequently quoted commentator on marriage on both sides of the Atlantic. She appears frequently on programmes in the UK, Australia and the US. She is an Affiliated Lecturer at Cambridge University and lectures to and trains mental health professionals in both the UK and the US.

Index

reading partner's mind 175, 178

reading partner's moods 73, 97

reciprocal acts, expressing gratitude through 108

recriminations 5, 75–6, 176

redundancy, coping with 160

reflective notions 30–31

reframing 76, 169–70, 189, 190

regimented marriages 127–8

relationships
destruction of 6
need for 33–7, 66
seeds sown in childhood 14
working at 70, 147

relaxation exercises 177

relocating frequently 127

respect, boundaries of 174

responsibility
and communication 188–9
denial of 175
for enacting the factors 188
sense of 140

retirement years 160

right, need to be 79–80

Rob and Jenny xiv–xv

Robert and Judith 85, 117

romance, importance of 23–4

Rose and Harry 193

Ruth 3

Sally and Paul 157

second chances 193–4

security
long-term 56
providing 116, 124–5
in relationships 10
sense of 56–7, 68

self-assessment see exercises

self-consciousness 30, 59, 70

self-esteem 17, 54

separation
caused by parental family illness 118, 153
caused by work 21, 109–10, 136–8
fear of 125
and individuation xix, 8, 30, 34

settling for less and less 7

sex
building up to 134
in child-bearing years 155
decline in frequency and satisfaction 83, 84
as expression of love 25
and gender divide 85
increasing sexual pleasure 134–5
in middle years 159
and protective function of love 80–86
rebuffing sexual overtures 119
talking about 83
test of sexual satisfaction 86